GOOD
HOUSEKEEPING

Easy
Meal
Prep

GOOD HOUSEKEEPING

Easy Meal Prep

THE ULTIMATE PLAYBOOK FOR MAKE-AHEAD MEALS

HEARST
HOME

CONTENTS

O h my gosh, what are we going to eat?" I'm a little chagrined to admit this was one of the first things I thought—maybe *the* first thing—when I learned recently that my husband, who is the head chef in our home, would be away for a while. If it were just me, I would happily nibble on cheese-and-deli-meat roll-ups with a salad thrown in here and there until his return. But the thought of serving up three healthy, hopefully tasty meals a day for our 11-year-old? Well, yes, it threw me into a panic. I needed a plan.

Lucky me, I work with a test kitchen full of chefs and experts whose mission is to help home cooks deal with this kind of meal-related stress. Inside this book, you'll find recipes that were developed using their best time-saving, flavor-building wisdom combined with their genius plan-ahead tips and tricks. This is not just a guide to meal-prepping—it is your solution for making every mealtime easy and delicious. Ready to get going? Here's what you need to know:

- Start with the no-fail primer on the basic meal-prepping techniques (page 8). Every recipe in this book can be made using each preparation style, so choose the one that best fits your schedule.

- Our 28-day meal plan (page 210) lays out when to make each dish so you get a feel for the rhythm of meal prepping. Once you get the hang of it, use the blank templates to create your own meal plans.

- To keep things interesting, we've paired recipes with "Same Ingredients, New Meal!" ideas, added flavor variations, and included quick instructions for turning leftovers into completely different dishes.

- Cheat sheets throughout ensure successful experimentation. They include reference charts (like the one on cooking any cut of beef perfectly, page 23), and "Easy as 1, 2, 3" guides (like the blueprint for building delicious grain bowls on page 180).

- Want gluten-free, keto or vegan options? Look for recipes with these icons below the ingredients for easy reference.

Vegan   *Keto*   *Gluten-free*

Our take on meal prepping lets *you* decide when to cook and allows room for creativity. I'm excited to start this meal-prepping journey together!

Jane Francisco
EDITOR IN CHIEF

QUICK START

Want to ease your way into prepping with one meal a day? These recipes are great options.

BREAKFAST

These grab-and-go solutions will make sure your day starts well.

- Make-Ahead Egg and Cheese Sandwich (page 60)
- Choco-Cherry Granola Bars (page 207)
- Spiced Plum and Quinoa Muffins (page 47)

LUNCH

Regardless of what you pick, these recipes focus on lean protein, healthy carbs and veggies.

- White Bean and Tuna Salad (page 99)
- Butternut Squash and White Bean Soup (page 71)
- Asian Steak Noodle Bowl (page 137)

DINNER

Dishes that are heavy on veggies aren't just super easy to prep ahead of time; they also make for light but filling dinners.

- Pork and Veggie Stir Fry (page 121)
- Crispy Caprese Cakes (page 184)
- Mini Meatballs with Garlicky Tomatoes (page 129)

SNACKS

A healthy spin on your childhood favorites is just what you need when the afternoon slump hits.

- Green Matcha Popcorn (page 200)
- Zucchini Tots (page 195)

MEALS THAT MAKE LIFE EASIER

W hat's for dinner?" Do these three words strike dread in your heart? And by the time you get home from work, make dinner, eat and clean up, it can feel like it's almost time to go to bed, right?

Enter meal prepping, a planning method that simplifies cooking and organizes it around your schedule, so you never have to scramble through a 16-step recipe when you'd rather have your feet up, dinner done and Netflix on.

Here are the three key elements to meal prepping like a pro:

1. BIG-BATCH COOKING
Make big, multi-serving recipes when you have time (like on the weekends) and store them for use later in the week or freeze them to use next week or month.

2. INDIVIDUAL PORTIONS
Divvy up portions into containers ahead of time so you can grab and go for breakfast and lunch.

3. PREPPED INGREDIENTS
Do a bunch of chopping, peeling, slicing or roasting beforehand and use those prepared components in recipes later on.

Though we believe that meal planning can make your life easier, healthier and happier, we also know that plotting out an entire week's worth of meals isn't always doable. Our goal in this book is to offer you the tools to reap the benefits of meal planning while also allowing for some flexibility. Meal planning doesn't need to be a rigid, restrictive way of doing things. The goal here is to empower you to plan your meals for the week, while also teaching you to improvise and riff on recipes based on the ingredients you have on hand. We want you to see recipes as simply collections of ingredients that can be used in endless variations to create satisfying meals.

THE BENEFITS OF MEAL PREPPING

Easy meal prep will save you time and money by simplifying and streamlining your cooking routines. Planning your meals also helps you reduce waste in the kitchen. You'll stress less because you'll be able to prepare more meals with less effort. And you'll know ahead of time what you'll be eating too—so you can eat healthier and avoid sad desk lunches or takeout dinners.

THE BEST FOODS FOR MEAL PREPPING

FROZEN VEGETABLES

Broccoli, Brussels Sprouts, Cauliflower,
Cauliflower Pizza Crust, Green Beans, Peas,
Riced Veggies, Veggie-based Tater Tots,
Veggie Pastas

LEAN PROTEIN

Beef, Chicken, Eggs, Frozen or Canned
Seafood, Grated Cheese, Pork, Reduced-
sodium Cottage Cheese, Skyr, Tofu, Turkey,
Unsweetened Greek Yogurt

PULSES

Beans, Chickpeas, Lentils, Peas

STARCHY VEGETABLES

Canned Pumpkin, Cassava, Parsnip, Potato,
Sweet Potato, Taro, Yuca

STIFF FRESH VEGETABLES

Bell Peppers, Cabbage, Carrots, Celery,
Radish

STURDY GREENS

Green Leaf Lettuce, Romaine (dress just
before serving)

WHOLE GRAINS

Barley, Buckwheat, Farro, Oats, Quinoa,
Sorghum, Wheat Berries

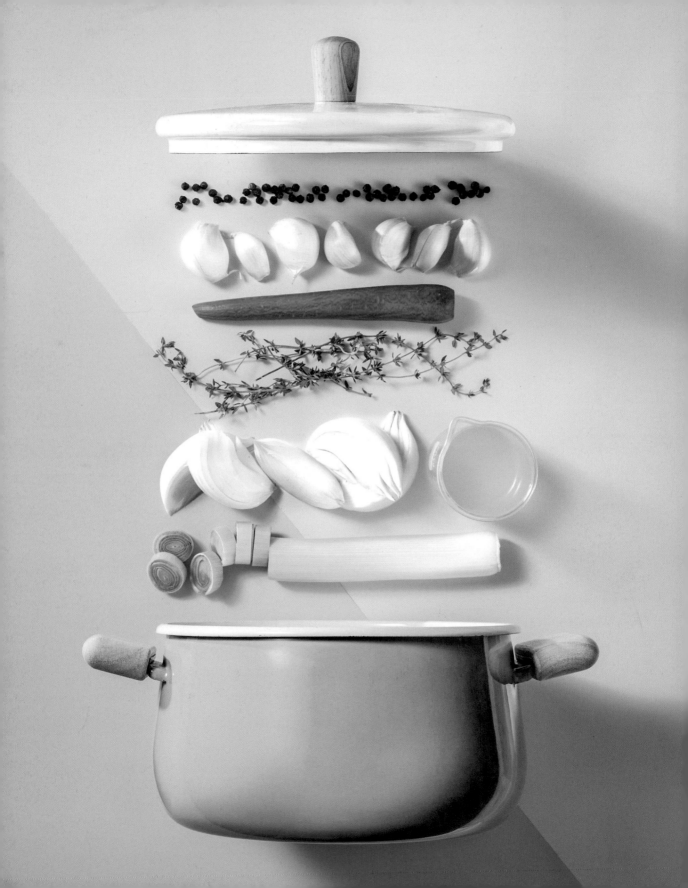

Big-Batch Cooking 101

Big-batch cooking, an integral part of meal prepping, simply means scaling up recipes (in many cases, doubling or tripling them) so you end up with multiple servings. From this point, you can portion what you've made to eat some now and store the rest for a later meal or to use in another recipe. In this first section of the book, we'll look at meal-prep essentials, like strategy and tools. You'll also find an easy reference guide for making big batches of staples like chicken, pork, beef, vegetables and grains, all organized by ingredient.

HOW MANY PEOPLE WILL A BIG-BATCH RECIPE FEED?

As many people as you need to feed. What qualifies as "big-batch" to you will depend on the number of people in your household, the size of their appetites and the amount of fridge and freezer space you have. Some of the recipes in this book make 2 servings, and some make 16 servings, but each of them is easy to scale up or down depending on your needs.

YOUR WEEK AT A GLANCE

Big-batch cooking works best when you apply a little strategy and plan in advance. You can divide your meal-prep week into four stages—planning, shopping, prepping and cooking:

PLANNING

Sit down and look at your calendar for the next week. Note which days you have already-scheduled plans for eating dinner or lunch out, or which weeknights will be particularly busy and will need a quick and easy dinner. Using your existing schedule, plot out what you'd like to eat each day. (Need some inspiration? Use our sample meal plans beginning on page 210 to get started and help you get the hang of planning.)

SHOPPING

Once your planning is complete, make a shopping list for everything you'll need. When you're at the grocery store, check labels for expiration or packed-on/use-by dates. Shop for packaged, canned or dry goods first, then head to the produce section to pick up your fresh fruits and vegetables. Lastly, grab cold/perishable items like meat, dairy and frozen foods. When you get home, refrigerate the perishable and frozen items first (put any raw meat on a plate to catch drips), and then put away the rest of your shopping haul.

PREPPING

Putting in a few hours up front to prep ingredients for future meals will save you tons of time on those busy weekday evenings when you need to get dinner on the table, stat. Many people do their prep work on a weekend day, but you can do it whenever you find yourself with a free block of time.

Prepping can include chopping all the vegetables for a week's worth of meals, cooking a big pot of beans or a double batch of rice, roasting a large piece of meat to use in several different dishes or putting together the ingredients for a multi-step dish to cook later. If you're new to meal prepping, you might want to start with prep for 2 to 3 days' worth of meals. Once you get more comfortable, you can prep for the whole week.

The recipes in this book will note which components can be prepped ahead.

COOKING

The cooking step can be as simple as reheating a dish you've made earlier, or it can involve spending 10 to 30 minutes transforming already-prepped ingredients into a quick dinner. Sometimes you'll be able to repurpose a part of a cooked dish into an entirely new meal. Since you've done the planning, shopping and prepping up front, the cooking step will be quick and easy.

Supplies & Tools

BAKING SHEETS

Heavy-duty rimmed baking sheets are essential for roasting vegetables and meat and making sheet-pan meals. Half-size baking sheets (18 by 13 inches) fit neatly in most home ovens, though quarter baking sheets (9 by 13) are also handy if you're cooking for a smaller number of people.

BOWLS

A set of nested stainless-steel or glass bowls can help keep your chopped ingredients organized while you prep.

CONTAINERS

Reusable, airtight food-storage containers keep food fresh longer and tasting better by locking bacteria and odors out. Choose the material (glass, Pyrex, stainless steel or hard plastic) and size that works best for you. Stackable, square or rectangular containers will maximize fridge space.

CUTTING BOARDS

Plastic cutting boards can be more thoroughly sanitized than boards made of other materials, meaning you can use the same plastic cutting board for both raw meat and fresh vegetables (after washing in between, of course). A board with a well near the outside rim is a good choice for cutting cooked meats (the well collects the savory juices). Wooden cutting boards are typically heavier, sturdier and more slip-proof, but also harder to clean.

DUTCH OVEN

A Dutch oven in the ballpark of 5 to 7 quarts is large enough to cook a whole chicken, a braise or a stew.

KITCHEN SHEARS

These heavy-duty scissors can perform all kinds of kitchen tasks, from cutting the backbone out of a chicken to removing the shells from shrimp to snipping small herbs.

KNIVES

A heavy, sharp 8-inch chef's knife is all you'll need for almost any prep work, but a 3- to 4-inch paring knife is helpful for smaller jobs like cutting fruit and peeling onions.

LARGE SKILLETS

A 12-inch skillet with deep or sloping sides is perfect for stir-fries, sautéing vegetables or searing smaller cuts of meat like chicken breasts or steaks. Make sure to have one that's oven safe as well as a nonstick. If you have a cover that can fit them, that is even better.

....

SAUCEPAN

A smaller saucepan (2 or 3 quarts) works well to reheat soups as well as to make rice or smaller quantities of pasta or grains.

....

STOCKPOT

An 8-quart pot is a great size for cooking pasta and grains, making soups and blanching vegetables.

....

TONGS

Tongs are perfect for flipping steaks, burgers and chicken breasts in a pan or on a grill. But they've got many other uses too: pulling food out of hot water (like boiled potatoes), tossing and serving salads or slaws, portioning out servings of pasta, or even squeezing juice from halved lemons or limes. You can find tongs with silicone handles and grips, but plain stainless-steel tongs work just as well.

Chicken

||||||||||||||||||||||||||||||||||||||||||||||||||||||||||||||||||||||||||||||||||||||||||||||||||||||||||||||||||||||||||||||||||||||||||||||||||||||||||||||

High in protein, fairly low in fat, pleasing to most palates, easy to store, chicken is a perfect protein for meal prepping. Here's everything you need to know.

BUYING, STORING AND COOKING CHICKEN

Look for chicken that's plump and meaty, whether you're buying a whole bird or parts. Skin should be smooth, moist, and bruise-free, and can range from creamy white to yellow (this depends on the breed of chicken and what it was fed). Use the sell-by date on the package as a guide — avoid buying any chicken that's near the sell-by date unless you plan to cook or freeze it immediately.

If you buy frozen chicken, avoid any packages with tears, freezer burn or frozen liquid in the bottom. (To thaw and cook frozen chicken correctly, see Freezer Guidelines, page 40.)

Store chicken in its original packaging or in a large plastic bag. Place it on a plate to catch any drips and put it on the bottom shelf of your fridge. Before you cook chicken, pat it dry with paper towels (to avoid cross-contamination, never rinse it).

MEAL-PREP STAR
WHOLE CHICKEN

Cooking a whole chicken (or two) is a simple way to get dinner on the table for tonight and then have the makings for meals later in the week (see Roast Chicken, page 140). The leftover carcass can even be turned into homemade chicken broth.

CHICKEN COOKING GUIDE

Cut	Methods	Cooking Tips	Recipe
Breast	Grill, sauté, roast, poach. Cook to 165°F and then let rest at least 5 minutes before serving.	Pound chicken breast flat between two sheets of plastic wrap for even, speedy cooking	Pan-Fried Chicken with Lemony Roasted Broccoli (page 149)
Ground	Sauté, grill (cook until no pink remains).	Season well (ground chicken has a very mild flavor), and cook at a low temperature to avoid drying out the meat	Mini Meatballs with Garlicky Tomatoes (page 129) — sub ground chicken or turkey for beef
Thigh/Leg	Grill, sauté, braise, roast. Cook to 165°F.	Buy bone-in, skin-on legs for best flavor and crispy skin when grilling or roasting	Sheet-Pan Chickpea Chicken (page 165)
Whole	Roast. Cook to 165°F and then let rest at least 10 minutes before carving.	Butterfly a whole chicken for faster roasting: Flip it over onto the breast side and use sharp scissors to cut out the backbone, then flip back over and press down with your hands to flatten out the meat.	Roasted Jerk Chicken (page 145)

PERFECT CHICKEN BREASTS, EVERY TIME

Chicken breasts cook up fast and are good blank canvases for marinades and dry rubs. Cooked chicken breast will last three to four days in the fridge. Here are three techniques you can use time and time again:

SAUTÉ

Season your chicken breast (look for small breasts, 5 to 6 ounces each) with salt and pepper or other spices of your choice, then heat 1 tablespoon olive oil in a large skillet on medium heat. Cook chicken on one side until golden brown and the chicken releases from the pan, 7 to 8 minutes. Flip the chicken, cover the pan, and cook until chicken is cooked through, 7 to 8 minutes more (it should feel firm to the touch or measure 165°F on instant-read thermometer).

ROAST

Heat oven to 400°F. Rub chicken breasts with olive oil and season with salt and pepper (or try the Ultimate Rub, page 39). Place on a foil-lined baking sheet and cook until just cooked through (it should measure 165°F on an instant-read thermometer), 18 to 22 minutes.

GRILL

Marinate your chicken breasts for at least 20 minutes and up to 2 hours (try Gochujang-Ginger Marinade, page 39). Brush off any extra marinade and then grill over medium-high heat, about 6 to 8 minutes per side.

> ## MEAL-PREP STAR
> ## TURKEY
>
> While chicken is a favorite for dinner plates (Americans consume more than 100 pounds of it a year!), don't overlook that other poultry option: turkey. Turkey has a richer taste than chicken but typically has less fat than beef, making it a good middle ground between the two. And you can find turkey in all the same cuts as you can find chicken: whole, breasts, thighs, ground meat. Try swapping ground turkey in for ground beef in the Mustard-Crusted Mini Meatloaves (page 135) or the Hearty Bean and Beef Chili (page 89).

MEAL-PREP STAR
EGGS

Everyone knows about eggs for breakfast, but in fact, eggs are a versatile, inexpensive and nutritious ingredient that can be employed for every meal of the day. Layer sliced hard-boiled egg on a sandwich or grate onto a salad or roasted vegetables for extra protein in your lunch, or add soft-boiled eggs to White Bean and Tuna Salad (page 99). Or get dinner on the table in 10 minutes by cracking eggs into a pre-prepped sauce for Plum Tomato and Eggplant Shakshuka (page 146), or pulling a pre-made Tuscan Sausage and Kale Frittata (page 61) from the fridge.

Pork

From a succulent and well-seasoned pork shoulder to a juicy, flavorful pork tenderloin, you can't go wrong putting pork into your meal-prep lineup.

BUYING, STORING AND COOKING PORK

When shopping for pork, look for fresh cuts that are pinkish white (though a slight gray tinge is OK). The flesh should be firm to the touch.

Pork loin will be lighter in color than pork leg or shoulder. (Smoked and cured pork, like ham or bacon, may be darker in color because of the curing process.)

Store fresh pork in its original packaging or in a plastic bag. Place it on a plate to catch any drips and put it on the bottom shelf of your fridge. Cook it within 2 days of buying. Cured pork will last longer, up to 2 weeks.

Cooking times depend on the cut. See the Cooking Cheat Sheet for details.

MEAL-PREP STAR
PORK SHOULDER

You may see pork labeled "pork shoulder" or "pork butt." In fact, both cuts come from the shoulder of a pig, and they both benefit from long, slow-cooking methods like roasting or braising. Cooking a pork shoulder is a great project to tackle on a prep day — you'll reap the rewards all week long. Try Cuban-Style Pulled Pork with Olives (page 114).

PORK COOKING GUIDE

Cut	Methods	Cooking Tips	Recipe
Butt/ Shoulder	Braise, slow cook, roast (25 minutes per pound at 350°F)	Cook whole in the oven, or cut into chunks and use in a stew	Citrusy Shredded Pork (page 123)
Chops (boneless or bone-in)	Grill or sauté (6 to 10 minutes for a ¾-inch boneless chop, 8 to 12 minutes for a bone-in chop). Cook to 145°F and let rest for 5 to 10 minutes before serving.	Sear pork chops on each side in a skillet, then transfer to a baking sheet and roast at 425°F	
Ground	Sauté, grill (until no pink remains)	Use ground pork in stir-fries in place of sliced meat	Mexican Beef Meatballs with Chipotle Sauce (page 134) – sub ground pork for beef
Loin	Grill, sauté, roast. Cook to 145°F (25 min per pound at 350°F) and let rest for 10 minutes before slicing.	Sear loin in a sauté pan and then finish in the oven (as for chops, above), or cut a whole loin into chops	
Tenderloin	Grill, sauté, roast. Cook to 145°F and let rest for 10 minutes before slicing.	Apply a dry rub or brine for maximum flavor. Roast at 425 to 450°F for 20 to 25 minutes.	Pork Tenderloin with Quinoa Pilaf (page 113)

Beef

Beef in all its forms is savory and satisfying, whether it's a perfectly seared steak, a juicy burger or a warming stew. A little also goes a long way: A few pieces of sliced steak or a couple of meatballs add a protein punch to a salad or grain bowl.

BUYING, STORING AND COOKING BEEF

There are numerous cuts of beef and many different cooking methods to suit them. But don't worry about learning them all. When you're buying meat, just tell your butcher what kind of dish you're hoping to prepare (a roast, a stew, a braise, a pan-fried steak), and he or she can recommend a good cut in your price range.

Whatever cut you buy, look for moist flesh and a pink-to-red color. Ground beef should be bright red, with no gray in it.

Store fresh beef in its original packaging or a plastic bag, on a plate on the bottom shelf of your fridge to prevent drips, and cook it within a few days.

Depending on the cut and your desired doneness, cooking temperatures will vary, but a good rule of thumb is to cook steaks and roasts to 145°F and ground beef to 160°F.

MEAL-PREP STAR
GROUND BEEF

From meatballs to meatloaf and burgers to tacos, ground beef is a versatile ingredient that makes meal prep a cinch. It works well in make-ahead dishes, and also cooks up incredibly quickly on those nights when you just need dinner on the table now. For two hearty options that make the most of ground beef, try Mexican Beef Meatballs with Chipotle Sauce (page 134) or Hearty Bean and Beef Chili (page 89).

BEEF COOKING GUIDE

Cut	Methods	Cooking Tips	Recipe
Chuck roast, brisket, short ribs	Braise, stew (40 minutes per pound at 300°F)	Bone-in cuts add flavor and body to braises and stews	Five-Spice Beef Stew (page 91)
Ground	Sauté, grill (cook until no pink remains)	Look for a ratio of 85% lean meat to 15% fat in your ground beef for juicy and flavorful finished dishes	Mustard-Crusted Mini Meatloaves (page 135)
Standing rib roast, tenderloin, rib eye, eye round, tri-tip	Roast (20 minutes per pound at 375°F)	Sear boneless cuts or smaller bone-in cuts on the stovetop first to achieve a nicely browned crust, then transfer to the oven to finish cooking	
Steaks: sirloin, NY strip, T-bone, porterhouse, London broil, flank steak, hanger steak, skirt steak	Grill, sauté, broil, roast. Cooking times will vary for different cuts of meat and different-size steaks—a good rule of thumb is 2 to 6 minutes per side for medium-rare.	Cook over medium-high heat to get a nicely browned crust (key to the most flavorful steak). For thicker cuts, sear until browned, then roast at 400 to 425°F to desired doneness. Let any steak rest at least 5 minutes before slicing.	Steak with Kale and White Bean Mash (page 133)

HOW DO I KNOW WHEN A STEAK IS DONE? The easiest way to check a steak for doneness is to cut into its center. But to test for doneness without cutting the meat, you can use the skin between your thumb and forefinger. Relax your hand and squeeze the skin: that soft and spongy feel, with little resistance, is a rare steak. Form your hand into a loose fist—the skin will be a bit springy to the touch. That's medium-rare. And a medium steak is a tighter fist—firm, with minimal give. For thicker cuts you can use an instant-read thermometer (rare: 120 to 130°F; medium-rare: 130 to 135°F; medium: 135 to 145°F; medium-well: 145 to 155°F; well done: 155°F and up).

Fruit & Vegetables

Fresh and cooked veggies bring nutrients, crunch and color to the meal-prep plate. And fruit can be so much more than a side dish or dessert filling, bringing sweetness to savory dishes or livening up morning oatmeal.

TEST KITCHEN TIP Avoid storing fruit and vegetables together. Many fruits give off ethylene gas, which acts like a ripening hormone and can speed up the ripening process of other produce.

CHOOSING AND PREPPING FRESH VEGETABLES

1	Look for firm vegetables that are heavy for their size, and leaves that are perky, not wilted. Avoid bruised or soft vegetables.
2	Store most vegetables in the crisper drawer. With the exception of lettuces, don't seal any vegetables in plastic bags — it will speed decay. Store garlic, onions, potatoes, tomatoes and winter squash at cool room temp. And keep onions and potatoes apart — proximity can cause them to spoil.
3	Just before using, rinse vegetables under cold running water. Remove any surface dirt with a soft vegetable brush. Swish leafy greens in a large bowl of cool water, changing the water several times.
4	Cut vegetables into uniform pieces to ensure even cooking.

BUYING FROZEN

Picked at their peak and flash-frozen, frozen vegetables and fruits are often more nutritious than fresh, especially when fresh goods aren't in season. Here are some great ingredients to buy frozen:

VEGETABLES

- Broccoli
- Corn
- Edamame
- Green beans
- Okra
- Onions
- Peas
- Potatoes (or French fries!)
- Spinach

FRUITS

- Berries
- Cherries
- Cranberries
- Mango
- Peaches
- Pineapple

Most vegetables are blanched (partially cooked) before they're frozen. Follow package directions, but as a general rule, add them frozen to your recipe, allowing them enough time to warm through. The texture of frozen fruits and vegetables can be a bit mushy once cooked, so use them in recipes like casseroles or soups, where their texture won't be an issue.

PERFECT ROASTED VEGETABLES, EVERY TIME

Vegetables especially benefit from the high, dry heat of the oven. Their flavor becomes concentrated and their natural sugars caramelize, transforming them into richly satisfying sides. For every 2 pounds of vegetables, toss with 1 tablespoon olive oil prior to roasting. Spread in a single layer on a rimmed baking sheet, with space in between the pieces so they caramelize well. Roast until tender and lightly browned, stirring once or twice during cooking.

If you are roasting a large amount of vegetables to use in your meal prep, divide them between two baking sheets. Overcrowding the vegetables will cause them to steam instead of roast.

Rotate pans between upper and lower oven racks halfway through cooking.

You can roast different veggies together if their cooking times are similar.

TOP IT OFF

Got small, leftover portions of roasted veggies? Turn them into filling, big-flavor toppings on build-your-own dishes like pizza, tacos (page 126) and grain bowls (page 180).

VEGETABLE ROASTING GUIDE

Vegetable	How To Cut	Roasting Time At 450°F	Flavoring
Asparagus	Trim	8 to 12 minutes	Sprinkle with lemon zest
Beets (without tops)	Whole, unpeeled, pricked with a fork, then peeled after roasting	1 hour	Peel, cut in pieces, season with salt, pepper and fresh orange zest
Broccoli	Trim and peel stem, split florets into 1½-inch-wide pieces	10 to 15 minutes	Sprinkle with grated Parmesan or extra-sharp Cheddar
Brussels sprouts	Trim and halved through stem end	15 to 20 minutes	Toss with maple syrup immediately after roasting
Butternut squash	Cut into 1-inch pieces	25 to 35 minutes	Toss with fresh thyme before roasting
Carrots	Peeled and halved or quartered lengthwise, if thick	20 to 30 minutes	Toss with ground cumin and coriander before roasting
Cauliflower	Cut into 1½-inch florets	20 to 30 minutes	Sprinkle with chopped fresh parsley and crushed red pepper flakes
Green beans	Trim	10 to 15 minutes	Toss with chopped fresh dill, tarragon or chives
Potatoes and Sweet Potatoes	Cut into 1-inch-thick wedges	25 to 30 minutes	Toss with fresh rosemary or coriander before roasting
Sweet peppers	Cut into 1-inch-wide strips	15 to 25 minutes	Toss with chopped parsley, a splash of vinegar and season with salt and pepper

Beans & Legumes

Beans and legumes are nutritional powerhouses. They're inexpensive; packed with B vitamins, fiber and other nutrients; and a protein-rich vegetarian and gluten-free option. Here are some of our favorites:

- Black beans
- Chickpeas (garbanzo beans)
- Kidney beans
- Lentils
- Pinto beans
- White beans (navy, cannellini, etc.)

COOKING BEANS FROM SCRATCH

While canned beans are a snap for meal prepping, dried beans are way easier to cook than you might think (and even cheaper than the canned version). And whipping up a big batch of beans on the weekend means you'll have beans for a whole host of meals in the week to come. See No-Fail Dry Beans on page 30.

COOL BEAN AND LEGUME DISHES

- Swap pasta for beans in your favorite recipe. For example, white beans tossed with sausage and broccoli rabe is just as delicious as the classic rigatoni — or replace the pasta in Creamy Lemon Pasta with Chicken and Peas (page 153) with your favorite beans.

- Stir a cup of cooked chickpeas or lentils into almost any vegetable or meat soup (like Beef and Quinoa Soup, page 76) for a protein boost.

- Smash beans and legumes into delicious dips, like Classic Hummus (page 203) or White Bean Mash (page 133).

NO-FAIL DRY BEANS

ACTIVE TIME: 20 MINUTES | TOTAL TIME: 2 HOURS 40 MINUTES, PLUS OVERNIGHT SOAK | MAKES 6 CUPS

INGREDIENTS

2 cups dry beans of any kind
6 cups water
4 cloves garlic
1 small onion
8 black peppercorns
2 bay leaves
Fresh herbs (such as parsley, thyme or anything you have on hand), optional
Kosher salt and pepper

DIRECTIONS

1. Rinse the beans: Place the beans in a colander. Pick out and discard any pebbles or pieces of dirt, then run under cold water to rinse. Set the colander in a bowl of water and discard any beans that float to the top (these might have air pockets where dirt or mold exists).

2. Soak the beans: We like an overnight soak, so place the beans in a container, pot or whatever you have room in the fridge for, and cover with at least 3 inches of water.

3. Cook the beans: Place drained soaked beans in a large saucepan and cover with 6 cups water. Smash the garlic and quarter the onion and place both in the center of a piece of cheesecloth. Add peppercorns, bay leaves and any fresh herbs, if using. Gather the corners together and tie everything up with twine or thread to make a bundle (or purse) and add to the pot.

4. Bring the beans to a slow simmer, partially cover and simmer, stirring occasionally, until the beans are tender, 1½ to 2 hours. If at any point you see any beans peeking through the surface of the liquid, add enough hot water to cover by ½ inch (without enough water, they could stick to the bottom or not cook evenly).

5. Remove and discard the cheesecloth bundle and strain the beans, reserving the liquid. You can use this starchy liquid in soups and stews and to thicken sauces. The beans are ready to be seasoned with salt and pepper and eaten or to use in other recipes.

PER SERVING: About 180 calories, 0.5 g fat (0.2 g saturated), 12.5 g protein, 3 mg sodium, 30 g carbohydrates, 10 g fiber

MAKE IT SNAPPY

For the least patient among us (we hear you!), an electric pressure cooker such as the Instant Pot is the best way to turn this pantry staple into weeknight dinner magic. Place your beans in a pressure cooker and cover with water; be sure not to go over the max quantity line. Add salt and other aromatics. Cook at high pressure for anywhere between 20 to 40 minutes depending on the size of the bean and whether or not you soaked them first. Allow the pressure to release naturally and drain right away.

WHEN DO I SALT MY COOKED-FROM-SCRATCH BEANS?

When it comes to salt, be patient before adding a dash (or five). Unless you're using a slow cooker or pressure cooker, wait to add salt until the beans are starting to get tender (as in, you can bite them without breaking a tooth, but they're not completely cooked through). This usually happens about halfway through the cooking time.

Grains

Grains can be used as a base for bowls or fried rice (see page 180), mix-ins for soups or as easy side dishes, salads and toppings.

KNOW YOUR GRAINS

Bulgur: Cracked wheat popular in Middle Eastern cuisine, bulgur's small kernels cook quickly and are a great sub for rice or couscous in any dish.

Couscous: Tiny balls of crushed durum wheat, quick-cooking couscous is technically a kind of pasta. It's a good base for stews or saucy meat dishes.

Farro: This ancient grain has a nutty flavor and chewy texture. Look for "pearled" or "semi-pearled" varieties in the grocery store—they will cook faster.

Oats: Choose old-fashioned rolled oats for baking or for making a quick morning oatmeal; steel-cut oats have a nuttier taste and chewier texture and take longer to cook.

Polenta: Polenta is coarsely ground yellow corn and, when cooked with liquid and seasonings, makes a rich, creamy porridge that pairs well with both meat and vegetable dishes. Grits are similar to polenta, but are usually made with white corn rather than yellow.

Quinoa: Quinoa is a powerhouse grain that's both filling and nutritious—it's a complete protein, which makes it great for vegan or vegetarian diets.

Rice: Rice comes in short, medium and long grain—the shorter the grain, the stickier the cooked rice. The two most common varieties are brown and white. White rice cooks faster, but brown rice is higher in antioxidants, fiber and vitamins. Rice is a versatile grain and a great base to build on.

GRAIN COOKING GUIDE

Grain	Grain to Liquid (cups)	Stovetop Instructions	Yield (cups)
Brown rice	1:2	Bring to a boil, then cover and simmer on low for 45 minutes, or until water is absorbed. Remove from heat and let stand, covered, for 10 minutes.	3
Bulgur	1:2	Bring water to a boil, then stir in bulgur. Cover and simmer on low until water is absorbed and bulgur is tender, about 15 minutes. Remove from heat and let stand, covered, for 10 minutes.	3
Farro	1:4	Bring water and ½ teaspoon salt to a boil. Add farro and cook, like pasta, until firm yet tender, about 30 minutes. Drain.	3
Polenta	1:3	Bring water and ½ teaspoon salt to a boil. Stir in polenta. Simmer on low, stirring frequently, until polenta is soft and thick, about 20 to 30 minutes.	2½
Quinoa	1:1.5	Bring to a boil, then cover and simmer on low until water is absorbed and quinoa is tender, about 15 minutes. Remove from heat and let cool for 5 minutes.	3
White rice	1:2	Bring to a boil, then cover and simmer on low for 20 minutes, or until water is absorbed. Remove from heat and let stand, covered, for 10 minutes.	3

TEST KITCHEN TIP These recipes can be doubled or even tripled—use the ratio of grain to liquid found in the chart to multiply recipes. To store, let cooked grains cool completely, then refrigerate in an airtight container for up to 5 days.

Flavor Boosters

Sauces, dressings, rubs and marinades add big flavor, and they're versatile. Think of them like pops of color to add to your larger palette of meats, vegetables, grains and legumes. A pesto, for example, can be stirred into pasta, used to top chicken, spread on a sandwich or mixed into a dip.

Many of these recipes will keep up to a week or more, so feel free to make them in big batches and store in your fridge to use as needed. These same tips and tricks also apply to store-bought condiments you may have lingering on your fridge shelves.

DOUBLE DUTY

Many sauces, dressings or marinades have multiple uses. Try these suggestions, or create your own!

VINAIGRETTE

Use to dress your green salad, plus:

- Repurpose as a marinade for grilled chicken
- Use as a sauce for fish or grilled vegetables (Honey-Thyme Vinaigrette, page 36)
- Toss with a pasta or grain salad for extra flavor

DRY RUBS

Spice up your grilled meat, plus:

- Stir a tablespoon of dry rub into a bowlful of cooked pinto beans
- Replace the salt, sugar and seasonings in Sweet and Spicy Nuts (page 204) with 3 tablespoons of Ultimate Rub
- Mix 2 tablespoons of rub with a stick of softened butter. Spread on bread or corn on the cob.

PESTO

Stir into pasta, plus:

- Drop a dollop onto grilled chicken or steak
- Spread on a sandwich instead of mayo or mustard
- Stir into yogurt or sour cream for a dip for veggies or chips

TOMATO SAUCE

Dress up your spaghetti, plus:

- Use for braising chicken or beef
- Stir into cooked white beans, top with grated mozzarella and bake for "pizza beans" (Easy Tomato Sauce, page 38)
- Combine 1 cup of sauce with ½ cup dry white wine and ½ cup water, bring to a simmer and then use the liquid to poach fillets of white fish

SALSA

A tasty dip for chips, plus:

- Pour a jar into a pan, turn the heat on low and use as a base for poaching eggs
- Use as a base for soup instead of sautéed aromatics (Easy Red Salsa, below)
- Add to a grilled cheese or use as a zesty topping for scrambled eggs

....

EASY RED SALSA

ACTIVE TIME: 25 MINUTES | TOTAL TIME: 25 MINUTES | MAKES 3 CUPS / 12 SERVINGS

INGREDIENTS

- 2 jalapeños (seeded for less heat if desired), finely chopped
- ½ small white onion, finely chopped
- 2 tablespoons fresh lime juice
- ½ teaspoon salt
- ¼ teaspoon pepper
- 1 pound plum tomatoes, halved, seeded and chopped
- ½ cup fresh cilantro leaves, chopped

DIRECTIONS

In large bowl, toss jalapeños and onion with lime juice, salt and pepper; let sit 10 minutes. Toss with tomatoes, then fold in cilantro.

PER SERVING: About 10 calories, 1 g fat (0.01 g saturated), 0.4 g protein, 80 mg sodium, 2 g carbohydrates, 0.5 g fiber

BASIL PESTO

ACTIVE TIME: 10 MINUTES | TOTAL TIME: 10 MINUTES | MAKES 1 CUP / 16 SERVINGS

INGREDIENTS

- 3 cups loosely packed basil
- ½ cup extra virgin olive oil
- ¼ cup grated Parmesan cheese
- ¼ cup toasted pine nuts
- 2 teaspoons fresh lemon juice
- 1 large garlic clove, crushed with press
- ¼ teaspoon pepper
- ¼ teaspoon salt

DIRECTIONS

In food processor or blender, pulse all ingredients until smooth. Keep refrigerated for up to 3 days.

PER SERVING: About 80 calories, 8.5 g fat (1 g saturated), 0.8 g protein, 25 g sodium, 1 g carbohydrates, 0.2 g fiber

....

MINT PESTO

ACTIVE TIME: 15 MINUTES | TOTAL TIME: 15 MINUTES | MAKES 2 CUPS / 6 SERVINGS

INGREDIENTS

- 1 cup packed fresh cilantro leaves
- ½ cup packed fresh mint leaves
- ½ cup shelled pistachios
- 2 jalapeños, seeded and chopped
- 2 tablespoons fresh lemon juice
- 1 clove garlic
- ½ teaspoon salt
- ½ cup extra virgin olive oil

DIRECTIONS

In food processor, pulse cilantro, mint, pistachios, jalapeños, lemon juice, garlic and salt until finely chopped, stopping and stirring occasionally. Pulse in oil until well combined.

PER SERVING: About 320 calories, 28 g fat (11 g saturated), 14 g protein, 215 mg sodium, 3 g carbohydrates, 1 g fiber

....

HONEY-THYME VINAIGRETTE

ACTIVE TIME: 5 MINUTES | TOTAL TIME: 10 MINUTES | MAKES 1½ CUPS / 6 SERVINGS

INGREDIENTS

- 2 tablespoons red wine vinegar
- ½ teaspoon honey
-   Kosher salt
-   Pepper
- 1 shallot, finely chopped
- 1 teaspoon fresh thyme
- 2 tablespoons olive oil

DIRECTIONS

In small bowl, whisk together vinegar, honey, salt and pepper to dissolve. Whisk in shallot and thyme. Let sit 5 minutes then stir in oil.

PER SERVING: About 45 calories, 4.5 g fat (1 g saturated), 0.2 g protein, 160 mg sodium, 2 g carbohydrates, 0.2 g fiber

TRY THIS

❈

Add a little spice to any dish with this variation on Basil Pesto: Omit cheese and lemon juice. Replace half of basil with cilantro and replace pine nuts with roasted unsalted peanuts. Add 1 tablespoon fresh lime juice, 1 teaspoon sesame oil, 1 teaspoon grated ginger, 1 small serrano chile (seeded and chopped) and ½ teaspoon salt.

LEMON BALSAMIC VINAIGRETTE

ACTIVE TIME: 10 MINUTES | TOTAL TIME: 10 MINUTES | MAKES 1½ CUPS / 16 SERVINGS

INGREDIENTS

- 1 cup extra virgin olive oil
- ¼ cup balsamic vinegar
- ¼ cup fresh lemon juice
- 2 tablespoons Dijon mustard
- 1 tablespoon sugar
- 1 teaspoon salt
- 1 teaspoon coarsely ground black pepper

DIRECTIONS

In large jar (at least 2 cups) with tight-fitting lid, combine all ingredients; shake well. Refrigerate until ready to use or up to 1 week. Bring to room temp and shake well before using.

PER SERVING: About 130 calories, 14 g fat (2 g saturated), 0.2 g protein, 165 mg sodium, 2 carbohydrates, 0.08 g fiber

---

EASY TOMATO SAUCE

ACTIVE TIME: 5 MINUTES | TOTAL TIME: 17 MINUTES | MAKES 3 CUPS / 12 SERVINGS

INGREDIENTS

- 1 28-ounce can whole tomatoes
- ¼ cup olive oil
- 4 garlic cloves, finely chopped
- 1 teaspoon fennel seeds, chopped
- ¼ teaspoon red pepper flakes, crushed
- 2 sprigs of fresh basil or oregano
- ¼ cup dry white wine (optional)

TEST KITCHEN TIP Use a nonreactive saucepan, made out of stainless steel, glass, clay or enamel. A reactive pan made out of aluminum or copper will react to the acids in ingredients like tomatoes, vinegar and wine.

DIRECTIONS

1. Carefully squeeze out and discard seeds from canned tomatoes, then return them to can with their liquid. Using immersion blender, blend tomatoes until smooth.

2. In a Dutch oven or saucepan, heat oil, garlic, fennel seeds and red pepper flakes on low until it starts to sizzle, about 5 minutes.

3. Add tomatoes to pan along with a couple of sprigs of fresh herbs (use whatever you've got: basil, parsley, oregano, etc.) and wine if you have it.

4. Simmer on low, stirring occasionally, for at least 10 minutes. Remove herbs, and it's ready to top off your favorite pasta.

PER SERVING: About 55 calories, 5 g fat (0.5 g saturated), 0.6 g protein, 75 mg sodium, 3 g carbohydrates, 1 g fiber

ULTIMATE RUB

ACTIVE TIME: 5 MINUTES | TOTAL TIME: 5 MINUTES | MAKES 1 CUP / 16 SERVINGS

INGREDIENTS

- ¼ cup brown sugar, broken up if in clumps
- 2 tablespoons salt
- 2 tablespoons ground coriander
- 2 tablespoons ground cumin
- 2 tablespoons garlic powder
- 1 tablespoon ground ginger
- 1 tablespoon smoked paprika
- 1 tablespoon black pepper
- 1 tablespoon cinnamon

DIRECTIONS

In medium bowl, stir together all the ingredients. Store in airtight container or resealable plastic bag for up to 6 months.

PER SERVING: About 25 calories, 0 g fat (0 g saturated), 0.5 g protein, 1 mg sodium, 6 g carbohydrates, 1 g fiber

---

GOCHUJANG-GINGER MARINADE

ACTIVE TIME: 5 MINUTES | TOTAL TIME: 5 MINUTES | MAKES ½ CUP / 1 SERVING

INGREDIENTS

- ¼ cup soy sauce
- 3 tablespoons gochujang (Korean pepper paste)
- 1 tablespoon brown sugar
- 1 tablespoon toasted sesame oil
- 2 garlic cloves, crushed with press
- 1 teaspoon ground ginger

DIRECTIONS

In medium bowl, whisk all the ingredients until smooth. Use this marinade with 2 pounds hanger or flank steak or 3 pounds chicken parts. In a large zip-top plastic bag or lidded container, toss the meat with the marinade and let rest at least 1 hour or up to 3 hours before cooking.

PER SERVING: About 50 calories, 2 g fat (0 g saturated), 1 g protein, 860 g sodium, 8 g carbohydrates, 0.25 g fiber

TEST KITCHEN TIP Marinades can also be used as sauces for finished dishes. If you've used your marinade on raw meat or fish, you'll just need to boil it for 5 minutes for food safety before you use it as a sauce.

Freezer Guidelines

The freezer is your friend when it comes to meal planning! Making a big-batch meal and then storing part of it in the freezer is a great way to set yourself up for easy meals on nights you're pressed for time.

These tips will help keep your freezer well-organized.

1. CLEAR A SHELF

Your freezer probably also holds other food you use on a regular basis (ice cream, frozen fruit for smoothies, etc.). Having one shelf that's dedicated to made-ahead meals will make it easy to store and find things.

2. PACK UP YOUR FOOD

First, let cooked food cool down (putting hot food in the freezer is a no-no). Then select your containers. You can use plastic or glass containers (as long as they have airtight lids) or even plastic zip-top freezer bags. Quart-size mason jars are great for soups and stews. It's helpful to divide your food into portion sizes that will feed your household so you'll only have to defrost what you need. Individual pieces of food (chicken breasts, hamburger patties, slices of pizza, etc.) can be wrapped tightly in plastic wrap and then in aluminum foil.

3. LABEL YOUR CONTAINERS

Here's a chef tip that's easy to adapt for home use: With a Sharpie, write the name of the dish and the date on a piece of masking tape, then affix the tape to your container before you put it in the freezer.

4. LAST IN, FIRST OUT

When you put a container of food in the freezer, place it at the back and move older food toward the front. Stack containers to maximize space, making sure you place them so you can see the labels and easily find what you're looking for.

FREEZING FRESH PRODUCE

If you've overbought at the grocery store and you know that you won't be able to use up fruit or vegetables before they start to spoil, a good way to prolong their life is to freeze them.

Berries are particularly good candidates for freezing. Stem or hull them, halve them if they're large, and freeze them in a single layer on a parchment-lined rimmed baking sheet until firm. Then transfer them to freezer-safe containers or plastic freezer bags.

To freeze vegetables, blanch them first: Cook them in rapidly boiling water (we salt our water too) for the recommended time or until just tender. Then cool them quickly in an ice-water bath and drain well. This slows or stops the action of enzymes that can cause loss of flavor, color and texture. Freeze them on baking sheets just like you did the berries, and then transfer to containers and return to the freezer. Cook frozen vegetables with or without thawing.

Vegetables and fruits will keep in the freezer about 8 months. For more, see "Buying Frozen," page 25.

HOW LONG WILL MEAL-PREPPED FOOD LAST?

Prepared foods can remain refrigerated for 2 to 5 days or frozen for 3 to 4 months, depending on the ingredients. To play it safe and avoid foodborne illness, keep food out of the "danger zone" — temperatures between 40°F and 140°F. Sealing food in airtight packaging or storage containers will not only keep bacteria out, but also protect the flavor and lock moisture in.

DEFROSTING

The safest way to defrost food (both raw meat or other ingredients, and cooked dishes) is to move it from the freezer to the refrigerator. Small containers can thaw in a few hours, while larger portions may take up to 24 hours or more. When defrosting anything that might leak or drip (like packages of raw meat), place it on a plate or tray before moving to the refrigerator. Once your food is defrosted, use it within a few days.

While the overnight thaw is the best and safest way to defrost frozen food, there are other methods if you are pressed for time. Your microwave should have a "defrost" setting—check your owner's manual for specifics. If it doesn't, microwave your food in short bursts on low until it thaws. You can also use the cold-water method to thaw smaller cuts of meat like chicken breasts or steaks. Place the meat in a zip-top plastic bag and squeeze out as much air as you can. Submerge the bag in a large bowl of cold water. Change the water every 30 minutes. Smaller cuts (about 1 pound) will thaw in an hour or less, while larger cuts that are 3 to 4 pounds can take 2 to 3 hours. If it's raw meat, cook it immediately (and thoroughly) after it thaws. Never try to defrost meat in hot water or at room temp. The FDA says this isn't safe.

Once you've thawed raw meat, proceed with your recipe as written. Or if you're thawing an already-cooked dish, reheat it in the microwave, the oven or on the stovetop.

HOW LONG CAN YOU KEEP MEAT IN THE FREEZER?

Meat	Freezer Storage
Ground meat *Beef, turkey, pork, lamb*	Up to 4 months
Raw sausage *Think Italian sausage*	Up to 4 months
Bacon	Up to 6 months *(Tastier before the 4-month mark)*
Chicken *Boneless, skinless breasts*	Up to 6 months *(Tastier before the 4-month mark)*
Chops *Pork and lamb chops*	Up to 6 months
Hot dogs	Up to 8 months *(Tastier before the 6-month mark)*
Fully cooked sausage *Think kielbasa and andouille*	Up to 8 months
Steak *Strip, flank, sirloin, hanger*	Up to 8 months *(Tastier before the 4-month mark)*
Chicken parts	Up to 9 months *(Tastier before the 6-month mark)*
Whole chicken	Up to a year

NOTE As long as meat is kept at 0°F or lower, it is safe to eat indefinitely. This chart shows ideal times from a quality perspective. All of the numbers above assume that items have gone into the freezer vacuum packed and sealed. And some might last even longer.

Tuscan Sausage and Kale Frittata, page 61

Breakfast

Spiced Plum and Quinoa Muffins

ACTIVE TIME: 20 MINUTES ✕ **TOTAL TIME: 50 MINUTES** ✕ **MAKES 18 MUFFINS**

INGREDIENTS

1¼ cups all-purpose flour

1 cup whole-wheat flour

⅓ cup white quinoa (raw)

1½ teaspoons baking powder

1 teaspoon ground cinnamon

½ teaspoon ground ginger

½ teaspoon baking soda

½ teaspoon salt

2 large eggs, beaten

1 cup plain full-fat yogurt

½ cup (1 stick) butter, melted

½ cup honey, plus more for drizzling (optional)

2 plums, 1 chopped and 1 thinly sliced, divided

DIRECTIONS

1. Heat oven to 400°F. Line 18 muffin-pan cups with paper liners.

2. In large bowl, whisk flours, quinoa, baking powder, cinnamon, ginger, baking soda and salt.

3. In a medium bowl, whisk eggs, yogurt, butter and honey. Fold egg mixture into flour mixture until just combined, then stir in chopped plum.

4. Divide batter among muffin cups (about ¼ cup each) and top each with a couple of plum slices.

5. Bake for 15 to 20 minutes or until a toothpick inserted into center of muffins comes out clean. Cool in pans for 5 minutes, then transfer to wire rack to cool completely.

6. Drizzle with honey, if desired, before serving.

PER SERVING: About 160 calories, 7 g fat (4 g saturated), 4 g protein, 200 mg sodium, 23 g carbohydrates, 1 g fiber

SAME INGREDIENTS, NEW MEAL!

It takes about 2 medium zucchini to make 12 ounces grated for this recipe. Buy 4 extra zucchini (6 total) and grate them all at the same time. Reserve 12 ounces for this recipe, and use the rest for Mustard-Crusted Mini Meatloaves (page 135) and Zucchini Tots (page 195).

Mini Sesame Zucchini Loaves

ACTIVE TIME: 30 MINUTES ✖ **TOTAL TIME: 1 HOUR 10 MINUTES** ✖ **MAKES 12 SERVINGS**

INGREDIENTS

- ⅔ cup extra virgin olive oil, plus more for pans
- 2 cups all-purpose flour
- 2½ teaspoons baking powder
- 1 teaspoon salt
- ½ cup granulated sugar
- ½ cup packed brown sugar
- Zest from 1 large lemon
- 2 large eggs, at room temp
- 2 medium zucchini (about 12 ounces), coarsely grated
- 1 cup walnuts, toasted and chopped
- 2 tablespoons white sesame seeds
- Butter, for serving

DIRECTIONS

1. Heat oven to 350°F. Oil three mini (3- by 6-inch) loaf pans.

2. In large bowl, whisk together flour, baking powder and salt.

3. In second bowl, combine sugars, then sprinkle lemon zest on top. Rub zest into sugars with fingertips, breaking up any clumps of brown sugar. Add eggs and oil and whisk until smooth. Stir in zucchini, then flour mixture. Gently fold in walnuts.

4. Divide batter evenly among prepared pans. Sprinkle tops with sesame seeds and bake until toothpick inserted in centers comes out clean, 35 to 40 minutes.

5. Cool in pans on wire rack 10 minutes. Run thin-bladed knife along edges of pans and unmold loaves. Cool completely on rack.

PER SERVING: About 330 calories, 19.5 g fat (2.5 g saturated), 5 g protein, 290 mg sodium, 36 g carbohydrates, 2 g fiber

TEST KITCHEN TIP If you prefer single-serving muffins for a grab-and-go breakfast, bake the batter in muffin tins instead of loaf pans.

BIG BATCH

Bake this beauty for brunch Sunday morning, then portion it out to reheat a square (or two!) for breakfast all week long. Bonus: The fresh blueberry syrup can stay in the fridge up to a week, and it is also delicious over pound cake or even ice cream.

Sheet-Pan Pancake with Blueberry Syrup

ACTIVE TIME: 20 MINUTES ✕ **TOTAL TIME: 35 MINUTES** ✕ **MAKES 12 SERVINGS**

INGREDIENTS

- 1 pint fresh blueberries
- 1 cup pure maple syrup
- 2¼ cups all-purpose flour
- 2 teaspoons baking powder
- ½ teaspoon baking soda
- 1 teaspoon salt
- 2¼ cups buttermilk
- 2 large eggs, at room temp
- ¼ cup sugar
- 1 tablespoon honey
- 1 teaspoon pure vanilla extract
- 4 tablespoons butter, divided
- Yogurt, for serving (optional)

DIRECTIONS

1. Place 18- by 13-inch rimmed baking sheet (half-size baking sheet) on the center rack of oven. Heat oven to 450°F.

2. In small saucepan, combine blueberries and syrup and cook on low until heated through, about 5 minutes. Keep warm.

3. In large bowl, whisk together flour, baking powder, baking soda and salt. In second bowl, whisk together buttermilk, eggs, sugar, honey and vanilla. Melt 3 tablespoons butter and whisk into buttermilk mixture. Pour the wet ingredients over dry ones and fold just until no traces of flour remain (batter will be lumpy).

4. Carefully remove hot pan from oven and swirl remaining tablespoon butter all over the bottom to melt. Immediately pour in batter and quickly spread it out evenly.

5. Bake until golden brown and toothpick inserted in center comes out clean, 13 to 15 minutes. Cut into pieces and serve immediately with warm blueberry sauce and yogurt, if desired.

PER SERVING: About 265 calories, 6 g fat (3.5 g saturated), 6 g protein, 370 mg sodium, 48 g carbohydrates, 1 g fiber

Super-Simple Summer Smoothies

ACTIVE TIME: 5 MINUTES ❊ **TOTAL TIME: 5 MINUTES** ❊ **MAKES 2 SERVINGS**

INGREDIENTS

2 cups (10 to 12 ounces) fresh summer fruit (blackberries, raspberries, hulled strawberries, chopped peaches and/or nectarines), chilled

½ cup plain yogurt

¼ cup milk (dairy or nondairy)

*with nondairy milk and yogurt

DIRECTIONS

1. In blender, puree fruit with yogurt and milk, scraping down sides as necessary, until smooth. If desired, make multiple batches and layer two flavors in each glass.

PER SERVING: About 115 calories, 3.5 g fat (2 g saturated), 5 g protein, 40 mg sodium, 18 g carbohydrates, 3 g fiber

BIG BATCH Triple the recipe and pour the leftovers into ice pop molds — perfect snacks for hot days!

TEST KITCHEN TIP Portion 2-cup servings of fruit into freezer bags so you can make smoothies at a moment's notice.

Pumpkin-Cherry Breakfast Cookies

ACTIVE TIME: 20 MINUTES   **TOTAL TIME: 45 MINUTES PLUS COOLING**   **MAKES 16 SERVINGS (4-INCH COOKIES)**

INGREDIENTS

- 2 cups whole-wheat flour
- 1 cup old-fashioned oats
- 1 teaspoon baking soda
- 1 teaspoon pumpkin pie spice
- ¼ teaspoon salt
- 1 15-ounce can pure pumpkin
- 1 cup melted coconut oil
- 1 cup packed brown sugar
- 1 large egg
- ½ cup roasted, salted pumpkin seeds
- ½ cup dried cherries

DIRECTIONS

1. Heat oven to 350°F.

2. In medium bowl, whisk together whole-wheat flour, oats, baking soda, pumpkin pie spice and salt. Set aside. In large bowl, with mixer at medium speed, beat pumpkin, coconut oil, sugar and egg until well combined; gradually beat in flour mixture, then pumpkin seeds and dried cherries.

3. Scoop onto large parchment-lined baking sheet to form 16 mounds, spaced 2 inches apart. Flatten into disks.

4. Bake for 20 to 25 minutes or until dark brown on bottoms. Cool on wire rack. Store in airtight container at room temp for up to 2 days.

PER SERVING: About 290 calories, 17 g fat (12 g saturated), 5 g protein, 135 mg sodium, 33 g carbohydrates, 5 g fiber

BIG BATCH Double this recipe, then wrap cooled cookies individually in plastic and freeze for up to 2 weeks. Reheat in a toaster until crisp.

PACK IT UP

If you need to leave the house
early in the morning, make a quick
breakfast you can take with you
and eat when you arrive at your
destination. In an 8- or 12-ounce jar
with a lid (old jelly jars work well),
layer the granola of your choice, plain
or flavored yogurt, and chopped
fruit. Seal the jar, and off you go!

Best-Ever Granola

ACTIVE TIME: 30 MINUTES · TOTAL TIME: 1 HOUR 15 MINUTES · MAKES 14 SERVINGS (7 CUPS)

INGREDIENTS

- ¾ cup pure maple syrup
- ½ cup extra virgin olive oil or extra virgin coconut oil (melted)
- 2 tablespoons turbinado sugar (we used Sugar in the Raw)
- 1 teaspoon salt
- 3 cups old-fashioned rolled oats
- 1 cup unsweetened coconut flakes
- ¾ cup raw sunflower seeds
- ¾ cup raw pumpkin seeds

DIRECTIONS

1. Heat oven to 300°F. Line large rimmed baking sheet with parchment paper. In large bowl, combine maple syrup, oil, sugar and salt. Add oats, coconut flakes, and sunflower and pumpkin seeds and stir to evenly coat.

2. Spread mixture onto prepared baking sheet and bake, stirring every 15 minutes, until granola is light-golden brown and dry, 45 to 55 minutes. Let cool completely.

PER SERVING: About 295 calories, 19 g fat (5 g saturated), 6 g protein, 140 mg sodium, 29 g carbohydrates, 4 g fiber

TRY THIS

Ginger-Pecan Granola: Omit pumpkin seeds and reduce sunflower seeds to ½ cup. Add 1½ cups raw pecans (roughly chopped). Bake granola per recipe instructions, tossing with 1½ tablespoons grated peeled fresh ginger (from one 2-inch piece) when it comes out of oven.

Sweet and Spicy Granola: Omit coconut flakes and increase pumpkin and sunflower seeds to 1½ cups each. Bake granola per recipe instructions, tossing with 1½ teaspoon ground cinnamon and 1 teaspoon chipotle chile powder when it comes out of oven.

BIG BATCH Double the recipe and store in an airtight container; it will keep up to 2 weeks.

Overnight Breakfasts

A make-ahead breakfast is a foolproof way to get your day started off on the right foot. Here are three easy recipes that can be prepped the night before and sit overnight. In the morning, they require only minimal effort (preheating the oven, for example) — or even none at all (just grab and eat!).

1 MINT PESTO BAKED EGGS

Grease six 10- to 12-ounce ramekins; place on rimmed baking sheet. To each ramekin, add **2 tablespoons heavy cream** and **2 eggs**; top with **1 tablespoon Mint Pesto** (page 36). Cover ramekins and baking sheet with plastic wrap, and refrigerate overnight.

In the morning, heat oven to 425°F. Bake 12 to 15 minutes or until whites are set but yolks still runny. Toast bread if desired. Serve eggs with extra Mint Pesto and toasted bread. Makes 6 servings.

2 MILK AND HONEY OVERNIGHT CHIA

To each of four 16-ounce jars, add **½ cup old-fashioned oats, 1 tablespoon chia seeds, 1 tablespoon honey** and **⅔ cup milk**. Cover; shake to combine. Refrigerate. Makes 4 servings.

3 OVERNIGHT STEEL-CUT OATS

Spray 4- to 6-quart slow-cooker bowl with nonstick cooking spray. To bowl, add **4 cups water**, **2 cups low-fat milk**, **1½ cups steel-cut oats** and **¼ teaspoon salt**; stir to combine. Program to cook for 4 hours on low and 4 hours on warm. Makes 4 servings.

Breakfast Burritos

ACTIVE TIME: 10 MINUTES ✂ TOTAL TIME: 35 MINUTES ✂ MAKES 4 SERVINGS

INGREDIENTS

- ½ pound tomatillos (about 4), husked, rinsed and halved
- 1 jalapeño, halved and seeded
- ½ small onion, cut into wedges
- ⅓ cup packed cilantro
- 2 tablespoons fresh lime juice
- ½ teaspoon salt, divided
- 6 large eggs
- 1 teaspoon extra virgin olive oil
- 1 cup grated pepper jack or Cheddar cheese, divided
- 1 cup fat-free refried beans, divided
- 4 large tortillas

DIRECTIONS

1. Arrange oven rack 6 inches from broiler; heat broiler.

2. Arrange tomatillos and jalapeño, cut sides down, on a foil-lined baking sheet along with onion, and broil until blistered, 10 to 12 minutes. Let vegetables cool, then transfer to food processor. Add cilantro, lime juice and ¼ teaspoon salt, and pulse to combine (salsa should be slightly chunky).

3. In medium bowl, beat eggs with 1 tablespoon water and the remaining ¼ teaspoon salt. Heat oil in large nonstick skillet on medium. Add eggs and cook, stirring with rubber spatula every few seconds, to desired doneness, 2 to 3 minutes for medium-soft eggs. Fold in ½ cup cheese.

4. Spread ¼ cup beans on each tortilla, then divide eggs and remaining cheese on top. Spoon 2 tablespoons salsa over each and roll, folding sides over filling and then rolling from the bottom up. If desired, crisp both sides in nonstick skillet on medium. Serve with remaining salsa.

PER SERVING: About 485 calories, 22 g fat (9.5 g saturated), 25 g protein, 1,340 mg sodium, 49 g carbohydrates, 4 g fiber

Make-Ahead Egg and Cheese Sandwich

ACTIVE TIME: 10 MINUTES ✕ TOTAL TIME: 10 MINUTES ✕ MAKES 4 SERVINGS

INGREDIENTS

- 4 large eggs
- ¼ teaspoon salt
- ¼ teaspoon pepper
- 1 tablespoon extra virgin olive oil
- 4 English muffins, toasted
- 2 ounces extra-sharp Cheddar cheese, grated, divided
- 2 cups baby spinach, divided
- 4 thin slices ham (optional)

DIRECTIONS

1. In medium bowl, beat eggs with 1 tablespoon water, salt and pepper. Heat oil in large nonstick skillet on medium heat.

2. Add eggs and cook, stirring with a rubber spatula every few seconds, to desired doneness — 2 to 3 minutes for medium-soft eggs.

3. Spoon eggs onto bottom half of each muffin and top with cheese, spinach and ham (if using). Sandwich with remaining muffin top.

PER SERVING: About 300 calories, 14 g fat (5.5 g saturated), 15 g protein, 540 mg sodium, 27 g carbohydrates, 2.5 g fiber

BIG BATCH Assemble as many sandwiches as you will eat in a month — they'll keep in the freezer for up to 30 days. Wrap prepared sandwiches in a damp paper towel, then foil. Place in freezer bags and freeze. When ready to cook, remove the foil (leave the towel) and microwave for 1 minute. Flip and microwave another 30 seconds to 1 minute. (The damp towel adds a touch of steam.)

Tuscan Sausage and Kale Frittata

ACTIVE TIME: 15 MINUTES ✖ **TOTAL TIME: 40 MINUTES** ✖ **MAKES 6 SERVINGS**

INGREDIENTS

12 large eggs

½ cup whole milk

½ cup grated pecorino cheese

½ teaspoon pepper

¼ teaspoon salt

2 tablespoons extra virgin olive oil

1 small onion, finely chopped

½ pound Italian sausage, casings removed

½ large bunch kale, stems discarded and leaves chopped

1 cup Easy Tomato Sauce (page 38) or jarred marinara

6 ounces fresh mozzarella, sliced

Fresh basil leaves, for topping

DIRECTIONS

1. Heat oven to 350°F.

2. In large bowl, whisk together eggs, milk, pecorino, pepper and salt.

3. Heat oil in large oven-safe skillet (preferably cast-iron) on medium. Add onions and cook, covered, stirring occasionally, until tender, 5 minutes. Add sausage and cook, breaking up with a spoon, until browned, about 5 minutes. Add kale and cook, stirring occasionally, until just wilted, about 1 minute.

4. Reduce heat to low and add egg mixture, stirring to distribute sausage and vegetables. Transfer to oven and bake until almost set, 18 to 20 minutes. Remove from oven and heat broiler.

5. Gently spread the sauce over the frittata, then top with mozzarella. Broil until cheese is browned and bubbling, 5 minutes. Top with basil and serve immediately.

PER SERVING: About 480 calories, 37 g fat (14 g saturated), 28 g protein, 835 mg sodium, 8 g carbohydrates, 2 g fiber

SAME INGREDIENTS, NEW MEAL!

Make extra mushroom ragu and toss it with pasta for a light dinner, or use it as a hearty vegetarian topping for a grain bowl.

Mushroom Ragu and Polenta Egg Bake

ACTIVE TIME: 20 MINUTES ✕ **TOTAL TIME: 1 HOUR 35 MINUTES** ✕ **MAKES 8 SERVINGS**

INGREDIENTS

- 3 tablespoons extra virgin olive oil, divided
- 2 medium shallots, finely chopped
- 4 cups chicken broth
- 1½ cups medium or coarse-grind cornmeal
- 1 teaspoon salt, divided
- 1 pound mixed mushrooms, sliced
- 2 cloves garlic, finely chopped
- 1 14-ounce can diced tomatoes
- 6 large eggs
- ¼ cup grated Parmesan
- Chopped parsley, for topping

DIRECTIONS

1. Heat oven to 350°F. Heat 1 tablespoon oil in 4- to 5-quart saucepot on medium. Add shallots; cook 3 minutes, stirring. Add broth and 3 cups water. Bring to a boil on high. Slowly whisk in cornmeal and ½ teaspoon salt. Reduce heat; simmer 4 minutes, whisking often.

2. Transfer polenta to 3-quart baking dish; cover with foil. Bake 45 to 50 minutes or until grains are tender and polenta has thickened, stirring every 15 minutes. Remove and discard foil.

3. Meanwhile, heat remaining 2 tablespoons oil in a 12-inch skillet on medium. Add mushrooms, garlic and the remaining ½ teaspoon salt; cook 10 minutes or until mushrooms have softened, stirring. Stir in tomatoes; cook 1 minute. Spoon mushroom mixture over cooked polenta.

4. Crack eggs and gently nestle into the mushroom mixture. Top each with a pinch of salt and pepper, then sprinkle Parmesan over top. Bake 20 minutes or until whites have set. Garnish with parsley.

PER SERVING: About 225 calories, 10 g fat (2 g saturated), 9 g protein, 790 mg sodium, 25 g carbohydrates, 5 g fiber

Spring Herb Frittata

ACTIVE TIME: 20 MINUTES ✕ TOTAL TIME: 40 MINUTES ✕ MAKES 4 SERVINGS

INGREDIENTS

- ¼ cup crème fraîche, at room temp
- 2 tablespoons chopped chives
- 6 large eggs
- 6 scallions, cut into 1-inch pieces
- 2 cups flat-leaf parsley leaves, plus more for sprinkling
- 2 cups cilantro leaves and tender stems, plus more for sprinkling
- ½ cup dill fronds, plus more for sprinkling
- 2 tablespoons tarragon leaves, plus more for sprinkling
- 4 tablespoons extra virgin olive oil, divided
- ½ teaspoon salt
- ½ teaspoon pepper

DIRECTIONS

1. Heat oven to 350°F. In small bowl, stir together crème fraîche and chives; set aside.

2. In large bowl, lightly beat eggs. Then, in food processor, pulse scallions, parsley, cilantro, dill, tarragon and 2 tablespoons oil until evenly and finely chopped. Add to bowl with eggs along with salt and pepper and mix to combine.

3. Heat remaining 2 tablespoons oil in medium ovenproof skillet on medium until shimmering, about 2 minutes. Add egg mixture and cook until edges have begun to sizzle and set, about 2 minutes. Transfer skillet to oven and bake until center is just set, 18 to 20 minutes. Let rest at least 5 minutes. Serve with chive crème fraîche. Sprinkle with more herbs, if desired.

PER SERVING: About 305 calories, 26.5 g fat (8 g saturated), 12 g protein, 375 mg sodium, 6 g carbohydrates, 2 g fiber

BIG BATCH Bake the frittata in a greased 9-inch square baking dish instead of a skillet (or pour the frittata mixture into a greased 12-cup muffin pan). Bake, let cool, then cut the finished frittata into squares and wrap in plastic. They'll keep two days in the fridge, and are delicious cold or at room temp.

Chicken and Red Plum Salad, page 105

Soups, Stews and Salads

TRY THIS

For an Italian-inspired soup, replace the jalapeño, ginger, coriander and cumin with 2 teaspoons dried oregano, and stir in ½ cup chopped fresh basil before pureeing.

Spiced Fresh Tomato Soup with Sweet and Herby Pitas

ACTIVE TIME: 10 MINUTES ✕ TOTAL TIME: 25 MINUTES ✕ MAKES 4 SERVINGS

INGREDIENTS

For the soup

- 2 tablespoons extra virgin olive oil
- 1 large onion, chopped
- 1 large red bell pepper, chopped
- ½ teaspoon salt
- 2 cloves garlic
- 1 jalapeño
- 1 1-inch piece ginger
- 2 teaspoons ground coriander
- 1 teaspoon ground cumin
- 2½ pounds tomatoes, roughly chopped
- 2 pocketless pitas

For the topping

- 1 tablespoon brown sugar
- 2 tablespoons butter or olive oil
- 2 tablespoons finely shredded unsweetened coconut
- 2 tablespoons cilantro

*without butter

DIRECTIONS

1. Heat large Dutch oven on medium-low. Add oil, then onion, red pepper and salt, and cook, covered, stirring occasionally, until tender, 8 to 10 minutes.

2. Meanwhile, finely grate garlic, jalapeño and ginger. Add to onion mixture and cook, stirring, 1 minute. Stir in coriander and cumin and cook for 1 minute.

3. Add tomatoes and 2½ cups water; increase heat and simmer, partially covered, 10 minutes.

4. While soup simmers, toast 2 pocketless pitas and make topping: In small bowl, combine brown sugar with butter, coconut and cilantro. Spread onto pitas, then cut in half to serve with soup.

5. Using immersion blender (or using a standard blender, working in batches), puree soup until smooth.

PER SERVING: About 325 calories, 16 g fat (6.5 g saturated), 6 g protein, 565 mg sodium, 43 g carbohydrates, 7 g fiber

BIG BATCH Double the soup recipe and keep in the fridge all week for an easy lunch.

SAME INGREDIENTS, NEW MEAL!

Buy 2 large butternut squash. Peel, seed and chop the squash into ½-inch pieces. Reserve one-quarter of the pieces for this soup, and use the rest for the Butternut Mole Enchiladas (page 179).

Butternut Squash and White Bean Soup

ACTIVE TIME: 20 MINUTES ⊠ TOTAL TIME: 45 MINUTES ⊠ MAKES 4 SERVINGS

INGREDIENTS

- 2 tablespoons extra virgin olive oil, divided
- 1 large butternut squash, peeled, seeded and cut into ½-inch pieces
- 1 onion, chopped
- 2 cloves garlic, finely chopped
- 1 1-inch piece fresh ginger, peeled and finely chopped
- 6 cups low-sodium chicken broth
- 6 sprigs fresh thyme
- 1 15-ounce can white beans, rinsed
- 1 15-ounce can chickpeas, rinsed
- ½ cup couscous
- ¼ cup roasted pistachios, finely chopped
- ¼ cup dried apricots, finely chopped
- ¼ cup fresh cilantro, chopped
- 1 scallion, sliced

DIRECTIONS

1. Heat 1 tablespoon oil in nonstick skillet on medium heat. Add squash and cook, covered, stirring occasionally, 8 minutes.

2. Meanwhile, heat remaining oil in Dutch oven on medium heat. Add onion and cook, covered, stirring occasionally, for 6 minutes. Stir in garlic and ginger and cook 1 minute more.

3. Add broth, thyme and butternut squash to onion mixture and bring to a boil. Using a fork, mash white beans and add to the soup along with chickpeas.

4. Cook couscous per package directions; fluff with a fork and fold in pistachios, apricots, cilantro and scallion. Serve soup topped with couscous mixture.

PER SERVING: About 560 calories, 15.5 g fat (2 g saturated), 26 g protein, 385 mg sodium, 88 g carbohydrates, 19 g fiber

MAKE AHEAD

This produce-packed soup lasts up to five days in the fridge, making it a great way to use up all your extra fresh veggies and also have a delicious, fast dinner any night of the week.

Spring Minestrone

ACTIVE TIME: 10 MINUTES ❊ **TOTAL TIME: 45 MINUTES** ❊ **MAKES 4 SERVINGS**

INGREDIENTS

2   tablespoons extra virgin olive oil

2   medium carrots, chopped

1   medium leek, thinly sliced

8   sprigs fresh thyme, tied together

½   teaspoon salt, divided

3   large red potatoes, chopped

2   quarts low-sodium vegetable or chicken broth

1   bunch asparagus, sliced

1   15-ounce can navy beans, rinsed (optional)

2   tablespoons chopped fresh dill

½   teaspoon pepper

*with vegetable broth

DIRECTIONS

1. Heat olive oil on medium in 8-quart saucepot. Add carrots, leek, thyme and ¼ teaspoon salt. Cook 8 minutes, stirring. Add red potatoes and broth. Partially cover and bring to a boil; reduce heat to simmer. Cook 25 minutes or until potatoes are tender.

2. Add asparagus and simmer 3 minutes or until tender. Discard the thyme. Stir in navy beans if using, dill, pepper and remaining salt.

PER SERVING: About 330 calories, 7 g fat (1 g saturated), 7 g protein, 1,030 mg sodium, 62 g carbohydrates, 7 g fiber

TEST KITCHEN TIP When you're slicing the asparagus, leave the stalks rubber-banded together. Trim the ends and cut through the rest of the stalk with a few quick strokes to slice all of your asparagus in seconds.

TRY THIS For a summer version of this minestrone, substitute chopped zucchini or summer squash for the asparagus, and garnish with chopped basil instead of dill.

Instant Pot Beef and Barley Stew

ACTIVE TIME: 25 MINUTES ⋇ TOTAL TIME: 55 MINUTES ⋇ MAKES 4 SERVINGS

INGREDIENTS

1   pound beef chuck, well trimmed and cut into 2-inch pieces

1   tablespoon all-purpose flour

1   tablespoon extra virgin olive oil

1   large onion, chopped

4   cloves garlic, peeled and smashed

8   sprigs thyme, plus leaves for serving

½   teaspoon salt

½   teaspoon pepper

1   12-ounce beer

½   medium butternut squash (1 pound), peeled and seeded, cut into 2-inch pieces

3   medium carrots (about 12 ounces), sliced

3   cups no-salt-added beef broth

1   cup pearled barley

DIRECTIONS

1. Set Instant Pot to "Sauté." In medium bowl, toss beef with flour. Add olive oil to Instant Pot, then cook beef until browned on all sides, 5 to 6 minutes. Transfer beef to a plate.

2. Add onion, garlic, thyme sprigs, and salt and pepper to pot, and cook, stirring occasionally, until tender, 5 to 6 minutes. Stir in beer. Press "Cancel."

3. Return beef to pot along with squash, carrots, beef broth and barley. Lock lid and cook on high pressure for 16 minutes. Then use quick-release method to release pressure. Serve sprinkled with additional thyme leaves if desired.

PER SERVING: About 485 calories, 9 g fat (2 g saturated), 35 g protein, 490 mg sodium, 67 g carbohydrates, 13 g fiber

TEST KITCHEN TIP   If you don't have an Instant Pot, use a Dutch oven or other large, heavy pot. Heat oven to 325°F. Follow the recipe through the first sentence of step 3, and then on the stovetop bring the stew to a boil and place the Dutch oven (covered) in the preheated oven. Cook, stirring occasionally, until meat is tender, 2 to 3 hours.

Freestyle Soups

Soups are soul-soothing dishes, and they're usually easy to make even without a recipe. Much of the time you need for a soup goes to hands-off simmering, so they are perfect to make on a weekend day when you're doing other meal prep or just want to relax on the couch with a good book.

IDEAS TO GET YOU STARTED

All it takes to craft delicious soup is to mix aromatics, veggies or meat, broth, mix-ins, and a final flavor boost. Try these simple combinations or follow the steps on the next page to create your own.

BEEF AND QUINOA SOUP

Carrot, Celery, Garlic, Onions • Diced Cooked Steak, Potatoes • Beef Broth • Cooked Quinoa, Frozen Peas • Chopped Parsley

BROWN RICE AND SPRING VEGETABLE SOUP

Shallots • Carrots • Vegetable Broth • Asparagus Tips, Cooked Brown Rice, Frozen Peas, Sliced Sugar Snap Peas • Parmesan Cheese

SPICY TOMATO SOUP

Onions, Garlic • Canned Whole Peeled Tomatoes • Chicken or Vegetable Broth • Red Pepper Flakes (puree soup in blender after simmering time) • Chile Oil, Minced Chives

STEPS TO GREAT SOUPS WITHOUT A RECIPE

Here's a simple blueprint for delicious soup every time.

1 AROMATICS

Sauté aromatics in oil or butter over medium heat in a deep, heavy pot. These diced vegetables form the base of your soup and give flavor that will perfume your entire dish. Try: **Carrot and Celery** · **Ginger, Scallions and Garlic** · **Onion, Celery and Green Pepper**

2 VEGGIES & MEAT

Add bite-size chunks of vegetables or quick-cooking meat, stir to coat, and sauté for 5 to 7 minutes to soften. Try: **Carrots** · **Chicken Breast or Thigh** · **Ground Beef, Chicken, Pork or Turkey** · **Kale** · **Peppers** · **Potatoes** · **Pork Tenderloin** · **Steak** · **Tomatoes**

3 LIQUID

Add stock or water. Cover the vegetables and other ingredients with liquid by about 1 inch, turn heat up to high, and bring to a boil. (Add salt to taste, especially if you're using a homemade stock.)

4 MIX-INS

Turn heat down to low, and simmer until vegetables and meat are tender and cooked through. At the end of the simmering time, **add any final fillers.** Try: **Asparagus** · **Frozen Peas** · **Precooked Grains** · **Precooked Pasta** · **Spinach**

5 FLAVOR BOOST

Top bowls of soup with **Grated Parmesan** · **Dollop of Plain Greek Yogurt** · **Pinch of Herbs** · **Swirl of Pesto** · **Sprinkle of Bacon**

SAME INGREDIENTS, NEW MEAL!

Buy and broil double the amount of vegetables. Use half the broiled vegetables for this recipe, and reserve half to make the sauce for the Enchiladas Verdes (page 159).

Fiery Black Bean Soup

ACTIVE TIME: 25 MINUTES ✕ **TOTAL TIME: 45 MINUTES** ✕ **MAKES 4 SERVINGS**

INGREDIENTS

For the soup

- ½ pound tomatillos (about 4), husked, rinsed and halved
- 2 cloves unpeeled garlic
- 1 large onion, cut into 1-inch-thick wedges
- 1 large poblano pepper, halved and seeded
- 1 jalapeño, halved and seeded
- 1 tablespoon extra virgin olive oil
- ½ teaspoon salt
- ½ teaspoon pepper
- ½ teaspoon ground cumin
- ½ teaspoon ground coriander
- 4 cups low-sodium chicken broth
- 2 15-ounce cans low-sodium black beans, rinsed
- 1 14.5-ounce can fire-roasted diced tomatoes, drained

For the pickled onion

- 1 small red onion, thinly sliced
- 2 tablespoons fresh lime juice
- Cilantro leaves, for serving

DIRECTIONS

1. Heat broiler. On large rimmed baking sheet, toss tomatillos, garlic, onion, poblano and jalapeño with oil, salt and pepper. Turn peppers cut side down and broil, rotating pan every 5 minutes until vegetables are tender and charred, about 15 minutes.

2. Once cooled, discard skins from poblano and garlic. Finely chop vegetables and transfer to Dutch oven to prepare soup. Add cumin and coriander and cook on medium, stirring occasionally, 2 minutes. Add broth, beans and tomatoes and bring to a simmer; cook 4 minutes.

3. Meanwhile, make the pickled onion: Toss red onion with lime juice and a pinch each of salt and pepper; let sit at least 10 minutes. Serve soup topped with pickled onion and cilantro.

PER SERVING: About 325 calories, 6 g fat (1 g saturated), 20 g protein, 705 mg sodium, 53 g carbohydrates, 18 g fiber

BIG BATCH Double the soup and freeze half in pint- or quart-size containers for up to two months. Thaw in the refrigerator overnight, then warm in a saucepan over medium heat until heated through. Prepare the pickled onions just before serving.

PACK IT UP

Double this recipe for a great healthy lunch you can eat all week long—it'll keep up to five days in the fridge. Cook and store the orzo separately (otherwise it'll soak up the broth and make the soup dry), and take a container of orzo and a container of soup with you to work or school. At lunchtime, combine the orzo and soup in a bowl and microwave until the soup reaches your desired temp.

Supergreen Mushroom & Orzo Soup

ACTIVE TIME: 5 MINUTES ✂ **TOTAL TIME: 35 MINUTES** ✂ **MAKES 6 SERVINGS**

INGREDIENTS

- 2 tablespoons extra virgin olive oil
- 1¼ cups chopped celery
- ½ cup chopped shallots
- ¼ cup minced garlic
- ¼ teaspoon salt
- 8 cups vegetable or chicken broth
- 3 cups chopped broccoli
- 3 cups sliced spinach
- 1 cup sliced mushrooms
- 1 cup orzo

Basil Pesto (page 36)

*with vegetable broth

DIRECTIONS

1. Heat oil in an 8-quart saucepot on medium. Add celery, shallots, garlic and salt. Cook 8 minutes or until golden, stirring.

2. Add broth and broccoli. Bring to a simmer. Reduce heat to medium-low; simmer another 15 minutes, stirring occasionally.

3. Add spinach, mushrooms and orzo. Simmer 8 to 10 minutes or until starches and veggies are softened.

4. Remove from heat and stir in basil pesto to taste.

PER SERVING: About 230 calories, 8 g fat (1 g saturated), 7 g protein, 360 mg sodium, 34 g carbohydrates, 5 g fiber

MAKE AHEAD

This veggie-packed ramen soup will keep in the fridge for up to three days. If you make it ahead, store the noodles, eggs and herbs separately, and stir them in just before serving.

Vegetable Ramen with Mushrooms and Bok Choy

ACTIVE TIME: 10 MINUTES ⁙ TOTAL TIME: 25 MINUTES ⁙ MAKES 4 SERVINGS

INGREDIENTS

- 3 scallions
- 1 3-ounce piece ginger, peeled and very thinly sliced
- 5 tablespoons low-sodium tamari or soy sauce
- 6 ounces ramen noodles
- 6 ounces shiitake mushroom caps, thinly sliced
- 2 heads baby bok choy, stems thinly sliced and leaves halved lengthwise
- 4 ounces snow peas, thinly sliced lengthwise
- 1 tablespoon rice vinegar
- 2 soft-boiled large eggs, peeled and halved
- ½ cup cilantro sprigs
- Thinly sliced red chile, for topping

DIRECTIONS

1. Slice white parts of scallions (reserve green parts) and place in large pot with ginger and 8 cups water; bring to a boil.
2. Stir in tamari, then add noodles and cook per package directions, adding mushrooms and bok choy 3 minutes after adding noodles. Remove from heat and stir in snow peas and vinegar.
3. Divide soup among 4 bowls and place 1 egg half on top of each. Slice remaining scallion greens and serve over soup along with cilantro and red chile.

PER SERVING: About 300 calories, 10 g fat (4.5 g saturated), 13 g protein, 1,075 mg sodium, 38 g carbohydrates, 4 g fiber

TRY THIS Add shredded chicken or sliced sirloin steak for extra protein.

Chickpea and Kale Soup

ACTIVE TIME: 25 MINUTES ✕ **TOTAL TIME: 25 MINUTES** ✕ **MAKES 4 SERVINGS**

INGREDIENTS

- 1 tablespoon extra virgin olive oil
- 6 cloves garlic, crushed with press
- 1 tablespoon finely grated lemon zest
- ¼ teaspoon to ½ teaspoon red pepper flakes
- ½ teaspoon fennel seeds, coarsely crushed
- 1 14-ounce can tomato puree
- 1 teaspoon salt
- 1 bunch Tuscan kale, stems and tough ribs removed, leaves coarsely chopped
- 1 15-ounce can chickpeas, rinsed
- ½ cup grated pecorino cheese

Lemon wedges, for serving (optional)

DIRECTIONS

1. Heat oil in large Dutch oven on medium. Add garlic and zest and cook, stirring, 1 minute. Add red pepper and fennel and cook, stirring, 2 more minutes.

2. Add tomato puree, 4 cups water and salt. Cover and bring to a boil; add kale and simmer for 4 minutes.

3. Add chickpeas and simmer until heated through, about 2 minutes more. Serve with pecorino and lemon wedges if desired.

PER SERVING: About 335 calories, 10 g fat (4 g saturated), 20 g protein, 695 mg sodium, 48 g carbohydrates, 11 g fiber

SAME INGREDIENTS, NEW MEAL! Buy 3 cans of chickpeas. Use 1 can for this recipe, and the other 2 cans to make Chickpea "Nuts" (page 196).

20-Minute Cauliflower Soup

ACTIVE TIME: 20 MINUTES ✖ **TOTAL TIME: 40 MINUTES** ✖ **MAKES 4 SERVINGS**

INGREDIENTS

For the soup

- 1 tablespoon butter
- 1 tablespoon extra virgin olive oil
- 1 medium onion, chopped
- 1 leek (white and light-green parts), chopped
- ½ teaspoon salt
- 2 cloves garlic, finely chopped
- 1 small head cauliflower (about 2 pounds), cored and sliced
- 4 cups low-sodium chicken broth
- ½ cup heavy cream
- Cracked pepper, for serving (optional)

For the chive oil

- 1 bunch chives
- ½ cup canola or grapeseed oil

DIRECTIONS

1. Heat butter and oil in large pot on medium. Add the onion, leek and salt and cook, covered, stirring occasionally, until very tender (but not brown), 10 to 12 minutes.

2. Stir in garlic and cook 1 minute. Add cauliflower, broth and cream and simmer until cauliflower is tender, 15 to 18 minutes.

3. Meanwhile, make chive oil: In blender, puree chives and oil until smooth. Transfer mixture to small saucepan and cook on medium until it begins to simmer, about 3 minutes. Pour hot mixture through a coffee filter set over a measuring cup to strain.

4. Using immersion blender (or standard blender, working in batches), puree soup until smooth.

5. Serve drizzled with chive oil and cracked pepper, if desired.

PER SERVING: About 245 calories, 19 g fat (10 g saturated), 8 g protein, 355 mg sodium, 14 g carbohydrates, 3 g fiber

White Bean Cassoulet with Pork and Lentils

ACTIVE TIME: 20 MINUTES ✖ **TOTAL TIME: 6 HOURS 25 MINUTES** ✖ **MAKES 4 SERVINGS**

INGREDIENTS

- 4 ounces thick-cut bacon
- 2 cups low-sodium chicken broth
- ½ cup dry white wine
- 3 tablespoons tomato paste
- 8 cloves garlic, peeled and smashed
- 1 medium onion, chopped
- 1 14.5-ounce can petite diced tomatoes, drained
- 2 pounds lean pork butt, trimmed and cut into 2-inch pieces
- 4 sprigs fresh thyme
- ½ cup dried brown lentils
- 1 15-ounce can small white beans, rinsed
- Crusty bread, for serving (optional)

DIRECTIONS

1. Place bacon on paper towel-lined plate and microwave on High until crisp, about 4 minutes. Cut into 1-inch pieces.

2. In 5- to 6-quart slow cooker, whisk together chicken broth, white wine and tomato paste. Add garlic, onion and tomatoes and mix to combine. Fold in pork, thyme and bacon.

3. Cook, covered, until pork easily pulls apart, 5 to 6 hours on High or 7 to 8 hours on Low.

4. Thirty-five minutes before serving, discard thyme, then gently stir in lentils. With slow cooker on High, cover and continue cooking until lentils are just tender, 30 to 35 minutes. Gently fold in beans and cook until heated through, about 3 minutes. Serve with crusty bread if desired.

PER SERVING: About 465 calories, 13 g fat (4 g saturated), 46 g protein, 775 mg sodium, 44 g carbohydrates, 13 g fiber

BIG BATCH This is a great stew to freeze. Double the recipe and freeze whatever you don't eat into appropriate-size serving portions for later.

Hearty Bean and Beef Chili

ACTIVE TIME: 25 MINUTES ✂ **TOTAL TIME: 40 MINUTES** ✂ **MAKES 4 SERVINGS**

INGREDIENTS

- 2 tablespoons extra virgin olive oil, divided
- 1 pound ground beef
- 2 teaspoons ground cumin
- 2 teaspoons chile powder
- ½ teaspoon salt
- ½ teaspoon pepper
- 1 onion, finely chopped
- 1 clove garlic, crushed with press
- 1 pound tomatoes, finely chopped
- 1 15-ounce can cannellini beans, rinsed

DIRECTIONS

1. Heat 1 tablespoon oil in large pot on medium. Add beef, cumin, chile powder, salt and pepper and cook, breaking up beef, until browned, about 10 minutes. Transfer beef to paper-towel-lined plate.

2. Return pot to medium; add remaining tablespoon olive oil, then onion, and cook until tender, 4 to 5 minutes. Stir in garlic and cook 1 minute. Add tomatoes and cook until they release their juices, about 5 minutes. Add 2 cups water and simmer until slightly thickened, about 10 minutes.

3. Transfer half the beans to small bowl and mash with fork. Add to pot along with whole beans and reserved beef and heat through.

PER SERVING: About 390 calories, 19 g fat (5.5 g saturated), 29 g protein, 483 mg sodium, 26 g carbohydrates, 11 g fiber

TEST KITCHEN TIP Toast up enough baked tortilla strips to give tonight's chili and tomorrow's salad a little crunch. To make: Heat oven to 425°F. Stack 4 small corn tortillas; thinly slice into ⅛-in.-wide strips. Arrange in single layer on large baking sheet. Spray all over with nonstick cooking spray. Bake 4 to 5 minutes or until deep golden brown. Let cool completely.

MAKE AHEAD

Soups and stews can be frozen up
to three months, then thawed in the
fridge overnight and reheated, covered,
on the stovetop. Simply add more
water or broth if it seems too thick.

Five-Spice Beef Stew

ACTIVE TIME: 40 MINUTES ✖ TOTAL TIME: 2 HOURS 30 MINUTES ✖ MAKES 6 SERVINGS

INGREDIENTS

- 2 pounds boneless beef bottom round, trimmed and cut into 2-inch chunks
- ½ teaspoon salt
- ½ teaspoon pepper
- 2 tablespoons canola or vegetable oil, divided
- 4 cups low-sodium beef broth, divided
- 4 medium shallots, quartered
- 3 cloves garlic, finely chopped
- 2-inch piece ginger, peeled and finely chopped
- 1 teaspoon Chinese five-spice powder
- 3 star anise pods
- 1 small cinnamon stick
- 2 tablespoons tomato paste
- 3 medium carrots, peeled and cut into 1-inch pieces
- 3 medium parsnips, peeled and cut into 1-inch pieces
- 2 small purple-topped turnips, cut into 1-inch pieces
- 1 15-ounce can crushed tomatoes
- 1 large bunch spinach, destemmed
- 2 tablespoons fish sauce
- 1 tablespoon fresh lime juice
- Cilantro and thinly sliced red chile

DIRECTIONS

1. Heat oven to 325°F. Season beef with salt and pepper. Heat 1 tablespoon oil in large Dutch oven on medium-high. Working in batches, cook beef, turning occasionally, until browned, 6 to 8 minutes. Transfer to large bowl; repeat with remaining beef.

2. Add ½ cup broth to pot and cook, scraping up any browned bits, 1 minute; transfer juices to bowl with beef.

3. Lower heat to medium and add remaining 1 tablespoon oil to pot along with shallots, and cook, stirring occasionally, until golden brown, 3 to 4 minutes. Add garlic, ginger, five-spice powder, star anise and cinnamon and cook, stirring, 2 minutes.

4. Stir in tomato paste and cook 1 minute. Return beef and juices to pot along with carrots, parsnips, turnips, tomatoes and remaining 3½ cups broth. Bring to a boil, then cover and transfer to the oven to bake until beef is very tender, 1½ to 2 hours.

5. Remove from oven and discard star anise and cinnamon. Stir in spinach, fish sauce and lime juice. Serve topped with cilantro and sliced chiles.

PER SERVING: About 365 calories, 12 g fat (2.5 g saturated), 41 g protein, 950 mg sodium, 28 g carbohydrates, 7 g fiber

Pressure-Cooker Winter Squash and Lentil Stew

ACTIVE TIME: 15 MINUTES ✂ **TOTAL TIME: 30 MINUTES** ✂ **MAKES 6 SERVINGS**

INGREDIENTS

- 2 medium shallots, thinly sliced
- 1 tablespoon finely chopped peeled fresh ginger
- 1 tablespoon vegetable oil
- 1 teaspoon ground coriander
- ½ teaspoon ground cardamom
- 1 small butternut squash, peeled, seeded and cut into 1½-inch chunks
- 1 pound dried green lentils, picked over
- 6 cups chicken or vegetable broth
- ¾ teaspoon salt, divided
- 1 5-ounce package baby spinach
- 1 tablespoon cider vinegar
- ½ teaspoon pepper

DIRECTIONS

1. In pressure-cooker pot on medium, cook shallots and ginger in oil, stirring, for 5 minutes or until shallots are golden. Add coriander and cardamom and cook 1 minute more, stirring. Add squash, lentils, broth and ¼ teaspoon salt.

2. Cover, lock and bring up to pressure on high. Reduce heat to medium-low. Cook 12 minutes. Release pressure by using the quick-release function.

3. Stir in spinach, vinegar, pepper and remaining ½ teaspoon salt.

PER SERVING: About 325 calories, 4 g fat (0 g saturated), 19 g protein, 705 mg sodium, 57 g carbohydrates, 15 g fiber

TEST KITCHEN TIP If you don't have a pressure cooker, use a stockpot or Dutch oven. Follow step 1, and then bring contents of the pot to a boil. Turn down to a simmer, and cook until squash and lentils are softened, 30 to 40 minutes. Proceed to step 3.

Kale and Roasted Cauliflower Salad

ACTIVE TIME: 20 MINUTES ✕ **TOTAL TIME: 40 MINUTES** ✕ **MAKES 4 SERVINGS**

INGREDIENTS

For the cauliflower topping

1   pound cauliflower florets

2   tablespoons extra virgin olive oil

⅛   teaspoon salt

⅛   teaspoon pepper

For the salad

¼   cup fresh lemon juice

3   tablespoons extra virgin olive oil

½   teaspoon salt

1   bunch kale, ribs removed, leaves chopped

¼   small red onion, very thinly sliced

⅓   cup crumbled feta cheese

⅓   cup golden raisins

⅓   cup toasted pine nuts

DIRECTIONS

1. Heat oven to 450°F. On large rimmed baking sheet, toss cauliflower florets with oil, salt and pepper. Roast for 25 minutes, or until stems are tender.

2. In large bowl, whisk lemon juice, oil and salt. Toss kale with dressing. Let stand at least 5 minutes.

3. To kale, add cooked cauliflower, onion, feta cheese, golden raisins and toasted pine nuts. Toss until well combined.

PER SERVING: About 370 calories, 28 g fat (5 g saturated), 10 g protein, 475 mg sodium, 27 g carbohydrates, 6 g fiber

MAKE AHEAD

All the vegetables for this salad can be chopped and portioned ahead of time and stored in the refrigerator overnight. You can also roast the squash and cook the couscous a day in advance; refrigerate separately for up to three days. Once tossed, the salad will last for a day in the refrigerator.

Roasted Squash Couscous Salad

ACTIVE TIME: 15 MINUTES ❊ TOTAL TIME: 35 MINUTES ❊ MAKES 4 SERVINGS

INGREDIENTS

1 medium butternut squash, peeled, seeded and cut into ½-inch pieces

2½ tablespoons extra virgin olive oil, divided

½ teaspoon salt

½ teaspoon pepper

1½ cups pearl couscous

2 tablespoons balsamic vinegar

2 teaspoons honey

½ small red onion, sliced

4 cups baby arugula

½ cup blanched almonds, toasted and chopped

½ cup pecorino cheese, shaved with peeler

DIRECTIONS

1. Heat oven to 450°F. On rimmed baking sheet, toss the squash with 1 tablespoon oil, salt and pepper. Roast until golden brown and tender, 20 to 25 minutes. Meanwhile, cook the pearl couscous per package directions. Drain and refrigerate until ready to use.

2. In large bowl, whisk together balsamic vinegar, honey and remaining 1½ tablespoons oil. Toss in red onion and let sit 5 minutes.

3. Toss couscous with onion mixture, then fold in squash, arugula, almonds and pecorino.

PER SERVING: About 620 calories, 21.5 g fat (4.5 g saturated), 21 g protein, 435 mg sodium, 89 g carbohydrates, 10 g fiber

White Bean and Tuna Salad

ACTIVE TIME: 25 MINUTES ✕ **TOTAL TIME: 25 MINUTES** ✕ **MAKES 4 SERVINGS**

INGREDIENTS

- 12 ounces green beans, trimmed and halved
- 1 small shallot, chopped
- 1 cup lightly packed basil leaves
- 3 tablespoons extra virgin olive oil
- 1 tablespoon red wine vinegar
- ½ teaspoon salt
- ½ teaspoon pepper
- 4 cups torn lettuce
- 1 15-ounce can small white beans, rinsed
- 2 5-ounce cans solid white tuna in water, drained
- 4 soft-boiled large eggs, halved, for serving

DIRECTIONS

1. Bring large pot of salted water to a boil. Add green beans and cook until just tender, 3 to 4 minutes. Drain and rinse under cold water to cool.

2. In blender, puree the shallot, basil, oil, vinegar, salt and pepper until smooth.

3. Transfer half of dressing to large bowl and toss with green beans. Fold in lettuce, white beans and tuna and serve with remaining dressing and eggs.

PER SERVING: About 340 calories, 16.5 g fat (3 g saturated), 31 g protein, 770 mg sodium, 24 g carbohydrates, 8 g fiber

Charred Shrimp & Avocado Salad

ACTIVE TIME: 10 MINUTES ✕ **TOTAL TIME: 25 MINUTES** ✕ **MAKES 4 SERVINGS**

INGREDIENTS

- 1¼ pounds large peeled and deveined shrimp
- 4 tablespoons olive oil, divided
- ½ teaspoon salt, divided
- ½ teaspoon pepper, divided
- ½ small pineapple, peeled, trimmed and sliced ½ inch thick
- 2 tablespoons fresh lemon juice
- ½ small red onion, thinly sliced
- ½ English cucumber, sliced into half-moons
- ½ bunch Upland watercress
- 1 avocado, quartered

DIRECTIONS

1. In large bowl, toss shrimp with 1 tablespoon oil and ¼ teaspoon each salt and pepper. Heat grill pan, grill or broiler. Brush pineapple with 1 tablespoon oil. Grill or broil (in batches on rimmed baking sheets) until pineapple is slightly charred and shrimp are opaque throughout, about 3 minutes per side on the grill or 6 to 8 minutes in broiler (rotating pan and turning food over halfway through).

2. Meanwhile, in another large bowl, whisk together lemon juice, remaining 2 tablespoons oil and ¼ teaspoon each salt and pepper. Toss with onion.

3. Once cool, cut grilled pineapple into smaller pieces. Add to bowl with onion along with cucumber and shrimp and toss to combine. Fold in watercress and avocado.

PER SERVING: About 420 calories, 23.5 g fat (3.5 g saturated), 35 g protein, 1,595 mg sodium, 20 g carbohydrates, 4 g fiber

SAME INGREDIENTS, NEW MEAL! Cook extra shrimp today and use it tomorrow for No-Cook Shrimp Rolls (page 171). Buy 2½ pounds of shrimp (instead of 1¼), and toss with 2 tablespoons olive oil and ½ teaspoon each salt and pepper. Grill or broil as directed, then use half the shrimp for this salad, and set aside and refrigerate the other half until ready to use (it will keep up to 2 days in the fridge).

Rotisserie-Chicken Cobb Salad

ACTIVE TIME: 20 MINUTES ✖ **TOTAL TIME: 20 MINUTES** ✖ **MAKES 4 SERVINGS**

INGREDIENTS

- 2 tablespoons extra virgin olive oil
- 2 tablespoons red wine vinegar
- ½ teaspoon salt
- ½ teaspoon pepper
- 2 plum tomatoes, diced
- 1 rotisserie chicken
- 1 avocado, diced
- 4 slices cooked bacon, broken into pieces
- ¼ cup crumbled blue cheese
- 4 thick slices iceberg lettuce, for serving
- 1 hard-boiled large egg, grated, for topping

DIRECTIONS

1. In large bowl, combine oil and vinegar with salt and pepper. Stir in plum tomatoes.

2. From rotisserie chicken, shred 3 cups of meat. Stir meat into dressing along with avocado, bacon and crumbled blue cheese.

3. Serve over 4 thick slices iceberg lettuce; top with grated hard-boiled egg.

PER SERVING: About 425 calories, 37 g fat (9 g saturated), 27 g protein, 955 mg sodium, 12 g carbohydrates, 5 g fiber

TEST KITCHEN TIP We get it—some nights you need your roast chicken served faster than it can take to cook from scratch. Enter the magical timesaver that is a rotisserie chicken. Available at many supermarkets, it'll allow you to get dinner on the table in mere minutes.

PACK IT UP

To make this as a for-later meal, follow the recipe as directed, but toss the arugula with the rest of the salad just before serving.

Chicken and Red Plum Salad

ACTIVE TIME: 20 MINUTES ✕ **TOTAL TIME: 20 MINUTES** ✕ **MAKES 4 SERVINGS**

INGREDIENTS

- 4 6-ounce boneless, skinless chicken breasts
- 2 tablespoons plus 1 teaspoon extra virgin olive oil, divided
- ½ teaspoon salt, divided
- ½ teaspoon pepper, divided
- 4 red plums, cut into 1-inch wedges
- 2 scallions, thinly sliced
- 6 cups baby arugula
- ½ cup fresh dill, very roughly chopped
- ¼ cup roasted almonds, chopped

DIRECTIONS

1. Heat grill to medium. Rub chicken with 1 teaspoon oil and season with ¼ teaspoon each salt and pepper. In large bowl, toss red plums with 1 tablespoon oil and remaining ¼ teaspoon each salt and pepper.

2. Grill chicken until cooked through, 5 to 7 minutes per side. Transfer to cutting board and let rest 5 minutes before slicing.

3. Add plums to grill and cook until just charred, 2 to 3 minutes per side; return to bowl and toss with remaining 1 tablespoon oil and scallions.

4. Add sliced chicken (and any juices) to bowl and toss to combine. Fold in arugula, dill and almonds.

PER SERVING: About 355 calories, 16.5 g fat (2.5 g saturated), 38 g protein, 345 mg sodium, 12 g carbohydrates, 3 g fiber

TRY THIS To save time, make this salad with leftover roast chicken or rotisserie chicken. And feel free to substitute other ingredients you like—peaches instead of plums, spinach instead of arugula, etc.

MAKE AHEAD

Buy 2 pounds of flank steak (and
double the marinade). Grill the steak,
and then slice half of it for the salad.
Refrigerate the second half of the
steak, and slice it as you need it
throughout the week to top grain
or noodle bowls (see page 180).

Korean Steak Salad with Sugar Snaps & Peanuts

ACTIVE TIME: 20 MINUTES ❁ **TOTAL TIME: 25 MINUTES** ❁ **MAKES 4 SERVINGS**

INGREDIENTS

¼ cup rice vinegar

2 tablespoons olive oil

2 tablespoons gochujang

1 tablespoon low-sodium soy sauce

Pinch sugar

1 1-pound flank steak

¼ teaspoon salt

¼ teaspoon pepper

8 ounces sugar snap peas

½ seedless cucumber, thinly sliced

6 radishes, thinly sliced

2 scallions, thinly sliced

1 head butter lettuce or Bibb lettuce, torn

Crushed peanuts, for topping (optional)

DIRECTIONS

1. Heat grill or grill pan on medium-high. In small bowl, whisk together the vinegar, oil, gochujang, soy sauce and sugar. Transfer 2 tablespoons of dressing to large bowl and set aside.

2. Season steak with salt and pepper and grill to desired doneness, 4 to 5 minutes per side for medium-rare, basting with dressing during last 3 minutes of grilling. Let cool before slicing.

3. In large bowl with dressing, toss snap peas, cucumber, radishes, scallions and lettuce. Fold in sliced steak and any remaining dressing and sprinkle with crushed peanuts if desired.

PER SERVING: About 300 calories, 15 g fat (4 g saturated), 27 g protein, 570 mg sodium, 14 g carbohydrates, 3 g fiber

Grilled Halloumi Salad

ACTIVE TIME: 20 MINUTES ✕ **TOTAL TIME: 45 MINUTES** ✕ **MAKES 4 SERVINGS**

INGREDIENTS

- 1   cup Israeli (pearl) couscous or quick-cooking farro
- 8   ounces asparagus, trimmed
- 4   ounces snap peas, strings removed
- 3   teaspoons olive oil, divided
- ⅛   teaspoon plus ¼ teaspoon salt
- ⅛   teaspoon plus ¼ teaspoon pepper
- 4½ ounces halloumi cheese, thinly sliced (about ⅛ inch thick)
- 1   teaspoon grated lemon zest plus 2 tablespoons lemon juice
- 1   scallion, thinly sliced
- ¼   cup fresh dill, chopped
- ¼   cup flat-leaf parsley, chopped

DIRECTIONS

1. Cook couscous per package directions. Drain, let cool and then transfer to large bowl. Heat grill to medium-high.

2. In second large bowl, toss asparagus and snap peas with 1 teaspoon oil and ⅛ teaspoons each salt and pepper. Grill, turning or rolling once, until lightly charred and tender, 2 to 4 minutes. Transfer vegetables to cutting board.

3. Grill halloumi until lightly charred, about 20 seconds per side. Transfer to plate.

4. Once cooled, cut asparagus into 1-inch pieces and snap peas into halves or thirds. Add to large bowl with couscous. Toss with lemon zest and juice, remaining 2 teaspoons oil and ¼ teaspoons each salt and pepper. Fold in scallion, dill and parsley.

5. Tear halloumi into pieces and fold into couscous.

PER SERVING: About 330 calories, 12.5 g fat (6.5 g saturated), 14 g protein, 525 mg sodium, 41 g carbohydrate, 4 g fiber

Crispy Caprese Cakes, page 184

Mains

SAME INGREDIENTS, NEW MEAL!

- Cook 2 cups of quinoa instead of 1½ cups, and reserve 1 cup cooked quinoa for the Crispy Tofu Bowl (page 175).
- Buy an extra ½ pound of pork tenderloin and use it for Pork and Veggie Stir-Fry (page 121).
- Save any leftover pomegranate seeds for Apple Snacks with Almond Butter and Pomegranate (page 201).

Pork Tenderloin with Quinoa Pilaf

ACTIVE TIME: 20 MINUTES ✕ **TOTAL TIME: 35 MINUTES** ✕ **MAKES 4 SERVINGS**

INGREDIENTS

- 2 tablespoons extra virgin olive oil, divided
- 1 clove garlic, thinly sliced
- 1½ cups quinoa
- 4 cups baby spinach
- 2 small pork tenderloins (about ¾ pound each), cut into 4 equal pieces
- ½ teaspoon salt
- ½ teaspoon pepper
- 2 tablespoons white wine vinegar
- 2 tablespoons orange marmalade
- 2 teaspoons Dijon mustard
- ½ cup pomegranate seeds, for topping

DIRECTIONS

1. Heat 1 tablespoon oil in medium saucepan on medium. Add garlic and cook, stirring occasionally, until toasted, about 2 minutes. Add quinoa and cook per package directions. Fluff with a fork and fold in spinach.

2. While quinoa cooks, heat a skillet on medium. Add remaining tablespoon oil, season pork with salt and pepper, and cook until browned on all sides and an instant-read thermometer registers 145°F, 12 to 14 minutes.

3. Meanwhile, in small bowl, whisk together vinegar, marmalade and mustard. Transfer pork to a cutting board and let rest 5 minutes. Discard any oil left in pan. Add mustard mixture to skillet and simmer until thickened, 2 to 3 minutes. Brush on pork.

4. Slice pork, serve over quinoa, and sprinkle with pomegranate seeds.

PER SERVING: About 545 calories, 16 g fat (3 g saturated), 45 g protein, 410 mg sodium, 54 g carbohydrates, 6 g fiber

Cuban-Style Pulled Pork with Olives

ACTIVE TIME: 25 MINUTES ✕ **TOTAL TIME: 3 HOURS 45 MINUTES** ✕ **MAKES 8 SERVINGS**

INGREDIENTS

- 2 tablespoons vegetable oil
- 2 medium green bell peppers, seeded and sliced
- 1 medium onion, sliced
- 3 cloves garlic, chopped
- ½ teaspoon salt
- 2 teaspoons ground cumin
- 2 teaspoons dried oregano
- 2 cups low-sodium beef broth
- 1 6-ounce can tomato paste
- 1 boneless pork shoulder (about 4 pounds), trimmed of excess fat and cut into quarters
- 1 cup pimiento-stuffed olives, sliced
- 1 tablespoon white (distilled) vinegar
- 8 cups cooked rice, for serving
- Cilantro leaves, for topping

DIRECTIONS

1. Heat oven to 350°F. Heat oil in a 6- to 7-quart oven-safe saucepot on medium heat. Add peppers, onion, garlic and salt. Cook 10 minutes, stirring occasionally. Add cumin and oregano; cook 1 minute, stirring.

2. In large bowl, whisk broth and tomato paste; add to pot along with pork. Heat to simmering. Cover and place in oven; cook 2½ to 3 hours or until pork is very tender.

3. Transfer pork to large bowl. Remove and discard fat from pork. Transfer vegetable mixture to a large fat separator; remove and discard fat.

4. With forks, shred pork and return to pot along with vegetable mixture. Stir in olives and vinegar. Reserve 3 cups pork mixture for empanadas, at right, if making.

5. Serve remaining pork with rice and cilantro.

PER SERVING: About 345 calories, 12 g fat (4 g saturated), 19 g protein, 1,065 mg sodium, 38 g carbohydrates, 2 g fiber

SAME INGREDIENTS, NEW MEAL! Turn pork leftovers into delicious and easy empanadas (see right).

Quick 'n' Easy Empanadas

INGREDIENTS

All-purpose flour, for dusting

1 17.3-ounce box puff pastry sheets, thawed

3 cups leftover Cuban-Style Pulled Pork with Olives

1 large egg, beaten

1 cup salsa verde, for serving

DIRECTIONS

1. Heat oven to 400°F. Line large baking sheet with parchment paper.

2. On a lightly floured surface, with lightly floured rolling pin, roll one sheet puff pastry into a 12-inch square. Cut it into quarters to form four squares. Trim corners off each square to form rough 6-inch rounds.

3. Scoop a heaping ¼ cup pulled pork onto center of each round. Wet edges of round with water. Fold each in half to form half-moons, pressing to flatten slightly and pinching and rolling dough to seal edges. Transfer empanadas to prepared baking sheet. Repeat with remaining pastry sheets and pork.

4. Brush empanadas with egg. Bake 25 minutes or until golden brown.

5. Serve with salsa verde.

PER SERVING: About 540 calories, 33 g fat (10 g saturated), 25 g protein, 1,095 mg sodium, 32 g carbohydrates, 3 g fiber

Sausage and Broccoli Quinoa Bowl

ACTIVE TIME: 10 MINUTES : **TOTAL TIME: 35 MINUTES** : **MAKES 4 SERVINGS**

INGREDIENTS

- 4   large Italian sausages
- 1   teaspoon plus 1 tablespoon extra virgin olive oil, divided
- 1   large broccoli crown (about 1 pound, cut into florets)

Kosher salt and pepper

- 1   cup red quinoa
- 1   cup plain yogurt
- 1   scallion, finely chopped
- ½   cup fresh mint, finely chopped
- 1   teaspoon finely grated lemon zest
- 2   tablespoons fresh lemon juice

DIRECTIONS

1. Place large rimmed baking sheet in oven; heat oven to 425°F. Prick sausages all over with knife. Toss with 1 teaspoon oil, place on heated baking sheet and roast for 5 minutes.

2. In large bowl, toss broccoli with remaining 1 tablespoon oil and season with salt and pepper. Add broccoli to baking sheet and roast, turning occasionally, until sausages are golden brown and cooked through and broccoli is lightly charred, 20 to 25 minutes. Transfer sausages to cutting board and slice when cool.

3. Meanwhile, cook quinoa per package directions.

4. In small bowl, combine yogurt with scallion, mint, lemon zest and juice. Spoon quinoa into bowls, top with sausages and broccoli and dollop with yogurt sauce.

PER SERVING: About 495 calories, 27 g fat (8 g saturated), 24 g protein, 670 mg sodium, 41 g carbohydrates, 7 g fiber

MAKE AHEAD Roast the sausage and broccoli up to 3 days in advance and store in the fridge. Cooked quinoa will also last up to 3 days in the fridge, so all you'll have to do is mix up the yogurt sauce and reheat the quinoa, sausage and broccoli before serving.

MAKE AHEAD

Ragu is the perfect hearty
make-ahead sauce because it can
be frozen for up to three months.
Thaw it in the refrigerator overnight,
reheat in a saucepan, and then boil
up the pasta and toss it all together
just before serving.

Pork Ragu Rigatoni

ACTIVE TIME: 25 MINUTES ✂ **TOTAL TIME: 25 MINUTES** ✂ **MAKES 6 SERVINGS**

INGREDIENTS

- 1 pound rigatoni
- 2 tablespoons extra virgin olive oil
- 1 large clove garlic, finely chopped
- 1½ pounds ground pork
- ¼ teaspoon salt
- ¼ teaspoon pepper
- 1 6-ounce can tomato paste
- 1 cup dry white wine
- ½ cup flat-leaf parsley, roughly chopped
- Shaved ricotta salata, for serving (optional)

DIRECTIONS

1. Bring large pot of salted water to a boil and cook rigatoni per package directions.

2. Meanwhile, heat oil and garlic in large skillet on medium 30 seconds. Add pork, season with salt and pepper, and cook, breaking up into pieces, until no longer pink, 5 to 6 minutes.

3. Add tomato paste and cook, stirring, 2 minutes. Add wine and simmer until it no longer smells like wine, about 5 minutes. Fold in parsley.

4. When pasta is al dente, drain and toss with ragu. Serve with ricotta salata if desired.

PER SERVING: About 615 calories, 26.5 g fat (7.5 g saturated), 33 g protein, 550 mg sodium, 59 g carbohydrates, 3 g fiber

MAKE AHEAD

Prep the carrots, peppers and onions and refrigerate in containers for up to two days.

Pork and Veggie Stir-Fry

ACTIVE TIME: 25 MINUTES ✂ **TOTAL TIME: 25 MINUTES** ✂ **MAKES 4 SERVINGS**

INGREDIENTS

1 cup long-grain white rice

2 tablespoons hoisin sauce

1 tablespoon fresh lime juice

1 tablespoon water

4 tablespoons canola oil, divided

4 ounces shiitake mushrooms, sliced

2 carrots, julienned

1 red bell pepper, thinly sliced

½ small red onion, thinly sliced

½ pound pork tenderloin, thinly sliced

¼ teaspoon salt

¼ teaspoon pepper

1 cup bean sprouts (optional)

Thinly sliced scallions, for topping

Toasted sesame seeds, for topping

DIRECTIONS

1. Cook rice per package directions. In small bowl, whisk together hoisin, lime juice and water; set aside.

2. Heat 1 tablespoon oil in large skillet over medium heat. Add mushrooms and cook, tossing occasionally, until golden brown and tender, about 5 minutes; transfer to a plate.

3. Add another 1 tablespoon oil to skillet, then carrots, bell pepper and onion and cook, tossing frequently, until vegetables are just tender, 4 to 5 minutes. Transfer to plate with mushrooms.

4. Heat remaining 2 tablespoons oil in skillet over medium-high heat. Season pork with salt and pepper and cook, tossing occasionally, until browned, 3 to 4 minutes. Add hoisin mixture and cook for 1 minute.

5. Return vegetables to skillet, add bean sprouts (if using) and cook, tossing, until heated through, about 2 minutes. Serve over rice and sprinkle with scallions and sesame seeds.

PER SERVING: 405 calories, 3.5 g fat (1.5 g saturated), 17 g protein, 305 mg sodium, 52 g carbohydrates, 3.5 g fiber

Sweet Potato, Avocado and Black Bean Tacos

ACTIVE TIME: 15 MINUTES ✕ **TOTAL TIME: 40 MINUTES** ✕ **MAKES 4 SERVINGS**

INGREDIENTS

1¾ pounds sweet potatoes, scrubbed and cut into ½-inch chunks

1 tablespoon olive oil

1 teaspoon chile powder

½ teaspoon salt

1 15-ounce can no-salt-added black beans, rinsed and drained

½ cup salsa verde

1 avocado, thinly sliced

8 corn tortillas

¼ cup crumbled cotija or feta cheese

Cilantro, for serving

DIRECTIONS

1. Toss sweet potatoes with olive oil, chile powder and salt. Arrange on large rimmed baking sheet; roast 30 minutes in 450°F oven.

2. In saucepan, combine black beans with salsa verde; cook on medium until warm, stirring.

3. Serve sweet potatoes and beans with avocado, corn tortillas, cotija or feta cheese and cilantro.

PER SERVING: About 465 calories, 16 g fat (3 g saturated), 13 g protein, 715 mg sodium, 70 g carbohydrates, 16 g fiber

Citrusy Shredded Pork

ACTIVE TIME: 15 MINUTES ✂ **TOTAL TIME: 6 HOURS, 15 MINUTES** ✂ **MAKES 6 SERVINGS**

INGREDIENTS

- ¾ cup fresh orange juice (from about 2 oranges)
- ¾ cup fresh grapefruit juice (from about 1 grapefruit)
- ½ cup fresh lime juice (from about 3 limes)
- 1 onion, finely chopped
- 1 habanero chile, seeded and finely chopped
- 1 bay leaf
- 2 pounds pork butt or shoulder, well trimmed and cut into 2-inch chunks
- 2 cloves garlic, crushed with press
- 1 tablespoon ground cumin
- 1 tablespoon smoked paprika
- 2 teaspoons dried oregano
- 2 teaspoons ground coriander
- 1 teaspoon salt
- ½ teaspoon pepper
- ¼ teaspoon ground cloves
- Tortillas and cilantro, for serving

DIRECTIONS

1. In a 6-quart slow cooker, combine orange, grapefruit and lime juices, onion, habanero and bay leaf.

2. Rub the pork with garlic, cumin, paprika, oregano, coriander, salt, pepper and cloves and place in slow cooker. Cover and cook until the pork is tender and shreds easily, 4 to 6 hours on High or 7 to 8 hours on Low.

3. When cooked, carefully transfer the pork to a bowl and shred with two forks, then toss with ½ cup cooking liquid, adding more if pork seems dry. Serve with tortillas and cilantro.

PER SERVING: About 220 calories, 11 g fat (4 g saturated), 22 g protein, 370 mg sodium, 8 g carbohydrates, 1 g fiber

BIG BATCH Double this recipe and keep it in the fridge all week long. Turn the pork into a filling for sandwiches, stir it into pasta, top a salad or grain bowl with it, or chop it and add to a vegetable soup.

TEST KITCHEN TIP If you don't have a slow cooker, combine all ingredients in a Dutch oven and cook at 300°F, covered, for 4 to 6 hours or until pork is fork-tender.

Carnitas Tacos

ACTIVE TIME: 20 MINUTES ✳ **TOTAL TIME: 7 HOURS 30 MINUTES** ✳ **MAKES 8 SERVINGS**

INGREDIENTS

- 1   tablespoon canola oil
- 4   pounds boneless pork shoulder, trimmed, cut into 3 pieces
- 2   tablespoons ground cumin
- 1   teaspoon salt
- 1   large white onion, chopped
- 3   poblano chiles, seeded and chopped
- 2   serrano chiles, sliced
- 4   cloves garlic, crushed with press
- ½   cup chicken broth or water
- ¼   cup fresh lime juice
- 24 small tortillas, warmed

  Cilantro, sliced scallions, sliced radishes, salsa and lime wedges, for serving

DIRECTIONS

1. Heat oil in a large skillet on medium-high until hot. Season pork all over with cumin and salt. Cook 5 minutes or until browned on two sides, turning over once halfway through. Transfer pork to slow-cooker bowl.

2. To skillet, add onion, chiles and garlic; cook 2 minutes, stirring often. Transfer to slow-cooker bowl along with broth and lime juice. Cover and cook on Low for 7 hours or until very tender.

3. Transfer pork to cutting board; with two forks, pull into bite-size shreds, discarding any fat. Serve with tortillas and fixings.

PER SERVING: About 430 calories, 14 g fat (4 g saturated), 36 g protein, 430 mg sodium, 38 g carbohydrates, 7 g fiber

Tacos

Tacos are about as versatile a meal as it gets. Choose a shell — think a classic tortilla or hard shell, or go outside the box with a lettuce leaf — and then fill it with the ingredients of your choosing. Roasted vegetables, shredded meats, slow-cooked beans, even leftovers from last night's dinner. Anything goes.

IDEAS TO GET YOU STARTED

Here are some winning taco combinations.

Flour Tortillas • Shredded Cabbage Dressed with Lime Juice and Salt • Halved Cherry Tomatoes • Shredded Rotisserie Chicken (left over from Enchiladas Verde on page 159) • Hot Sauce

Lettuce Leaves • Roasted Corn Kernels • Chopped Avocado • Shrimp Marinated in Lime Juice, Cilantro, Garlic and Cumin, and Grilled (or use leftovers from No-Cook Shrimp Rolls, page 171) • Cilantro Sprigs

Crunchy Taco Shell • Ground Turkey Cooked with Cumin, Oregano and Chile Powder • Shredded Lettuce • Guacamole • Pico de Gallo

Corn Tortillas • Pickled Carrots • Sliced Radishes • Pulled Pork • Crumbled Feta Cheese (left over from Kale and Roasted Cauliflower Salad, page 95)

BUILD THE PERFECT TACO

Mix and match these five elements for tasty tacos, stat!

1 SHELL
Crunchy Taco Shells • Lettuce or Kale Leaves •
Pita or Naan Bread • Pizza Crust • Potato Skins •
Seaweed Sheets • Soft Corn or Flour Tortillas

2 VEGGIES
Bell Pepper • Coleslaw • Grilled or Roasted
Jalapeño Pepper • Grilled Zucchini or Eggplant •
Halved Cherry Tomatoes • Pickled or Raw Sliced
Red Onions • Roasted Mushrooms • Roasted Sweet
Potato or Butternut Squash • Shredded Cabbage
or Lettuce • Sliced Avocado • Sliced Radishes

3 PROTEINS
Baked or Grilled Fish • Beans • Chickpeas • Fried
Tofu • Lentils • Ground Beef, Pork or Turkey •
Pulled or Shredded Pork • Rotisserie Chicken •
Scrambled or Fried Eggs • Sliced Grilled or
Roasted Chicken • Sliced Seared or Grilled Steak

4 TOPPINGS
Brown or White Rice • Cilantro • Chopped Mango
or Pineapple • Grated or Crumbled Cheese •
Kimchi • Minced Scallions • Olives

5 SAUCES
Guacamole • Plain Yogurt • Salsas • Sour Cream •
Squeeze of Lime

MAKE AHEAD

Cook the meatballs and refrigerate for up to four days. Warm in the microwave or oven along with the tomatoes.

Mini Meatballs with Garlicky Tomatoes

ACTIVE TIME: 45 MINUTES ✂ **TOTAL TIME: 45 MINUTES** ✂ **MAKES 4 SERVINGS**

INGREDIENTS

- 1 3-inch piece baguette (about 1 ounce)
- 2 large eggs
- 4 cloves garlic, 2 finely chopped and 2 crushed with press, divided
- 2 cups packed baby spinach, 1 cup finely chopped and 1 cup finely sliced, divided
- ¼ cup finely grated Parmesan
- ½ teaspoon dried oregano
- ½ teaspoon salt
- ½ teaspoon pepper
- 1 pound ground beef
- 1 pound Campari tomatoes, halved
- 1 tablespoon extra virgin olive oil

DIRECTIONS

1. Tear the baguette into pieces and soak in ¼ cup water until absorbed, then squeeze out all moisture and transfer to large bowl. Add eggs, chopped garlic, chopped spinach, Parmesan, oregano, salt and pepper and mix to combine. Add beef and mix until combined.

2. Heat broiler and line a rimmed baking sheet with nonstick foil. Shape mixture into tiny balls (about 1 level teaspoon each, about 92 balls) and place on prepared baking sheet. Broil until browned, 6 to 8 minutes.

3. Arrange tomatoes, cut sides up, on second baking sheet. Drizzle with oil and sprinkle tops with pressed garlic and pinch each salt and pepper. Broil until garlic is fragrant, 3 to 4 minutes. Serve meatballs with tomatoes and sliced spinach.

PER SERVING: About 310 calories, 16.5 g fat (5.5 g saturated), 29 g protein, 505 mg sodium, 11 g carbohydrates, 2 g fiber

SAME INGREDIENTS, NEW MEAL!

Double the amount of rice you cook and store what you don't eat in the fridge for Vegetarian Fried Rice with Shiitakes and Edamame (page 185).

Beef and Pineapple Kebabs with Cashew Rice

ACTIVE TIME: 20 MINUTES ⁑ TOTAL TIME: 25 MINUTES ⁑ MAKES 4 SERVINGS

INGREDIENTS

1¼ cups basmati rice

2 tablespoons soy sauce

2 tablespoons maple syrup

2 tablespoons rice vinegar

½ small pineapple, peeled, cored and cut into chunks

1¼ pounds sirloin steak, cut into 1½-inch chunks

4 large fresno chiles, each cut into 6 pieces

Extra virgin olive oil, for brushing

¼ teaspoon salt

¼ teaspoon pepper

⅓ cup roasted salted cashews, roughly chopped

¼ cup cilantro, chopped

2 tablespoons fresh lime juice

DIRECTIONS

1. Cook rice per package directions. Heat grill on medium-high. In small bowl, combine soy sauce, maple syrup and vinegar; set aside.

2. Thread pineapple chunks onto skewers. Thread sirloin steak chunks and chiles onto other skewers; brush with oil and season with salt and pepper.

3. Grill kebabs, turning occasionally, 4 minutes. Brush with sauce and grill until pineapple is lightly charred, 2 minutes, and steak reaches desired doneness, 3 to 4 minutes for medium-rare. Transfer to plates.

4. Fluff rice. Fold in cashews, cilantro and lime juice. Serve with kebabs.

PER SERVING: About 645 calories, 19.5 g fat (5.5 g saturated), 40 g protein, 480 mg sodium, 50 g carbohydrates, 2 g fiber

SAME INGREDIENTS, NEW MEAL!

Buy extra kale and use it for Tuscan Sausage and Kale Frittata (page 61), Kale and Roasted Cauliflower Salad (page 95), or Chickpea and Kale Soup (page 84).

Steak with Kale and White Bean Mash

ACTIVE TIME: 20 MINUTES ✂ **TOTAL TIME: 20 MINUTES** ✂ **MAKES 4 SERVINGS**

INGREDIENTS

- 2 8-ounce strip steaks, trimmed
- ½ teaspoon plus ⅛ teaspoon salt, divided
- ¼ teaspoon pepper
- 2 medium parsnips, thinly sliced
- 1 bunch kale, chopped
- 2 cloves garlic, chopped
- 2 15-ounce cans cannellini beans, rinsed
- 2 tablespoons Basil Pesto (page 36)

DIRECTIONS

1. Season steaks with ¼ teaspoon each salt and pepper; cook on grill pan on medium-high, 4 minutes per side for medium doneness. Transfer to cutting board; let stand 5 minutes.

2. Place parsnips and ½ cup water in a bowl; cover with vented plastic. Microwave on High 5 minutes or until very tender.

3. Spray large saucepot with cooking spray; cook kale, garlic and ¼ teaspoon salt on medium 5 minutes or until stems are tender.

4. Transfer parsnips to a food processor along with cannellini beans. Pulse until combined but still chunky, scraping sides of processor occasionally; stir into kale along with remaining ⅛ teaspoon salt. Heat through.

5. Thinly slice steak; top with pesto. Serve with mash.

PER SERVING: About 525 calories, 18 g fat (5 g saturated), 43 g protein, 775 mg sodium, 50 g carbohydrates, 20 g fiber

Mexican Beef Meatballs with Chipotle Sauce

ACTIVE TIME: 30 MINUTES ✕ TOTAL TIME: 30 MINUTES ✕ MAKES 4 SERVINGS

INGREDIENTS

1   cup long-grain rice

1   large egg

½   teaspoon ground cumin

½   teaspoon ground coriander

½   teaspoon salt

½   teaspoon pepper

2   cloves garlic, crushed with press

½   cup cilantro, chopped, plus more for topping

1   cup unsalted tortilla chips, crushed (about ½ cup)

½   pound ground beef

1   15-ounce can lentils, rinsed

2   cups jarred marinara

1   chopped chipotle in adobo, plus 1 teaspoon adobo sauce

Lime wedges, for serving

DIRECTIONS

1. Cook rice per package directions.

2. In large bowl, whisk together egg, cumin, coriander, salt and pepper. Stir in garlic, cilantro and tortilla chips. Mix in ground beef and lentils.

3. Heat broiler and line a rimmed baking sheet with nonstick foil. Shape mixture into 20 balls (about 1 inch each) and place on prepared baking sheet. Broil on middle rack until cooked through, 6 to 8 minutes.

4. Meanwhile, in medium saucepan, heat marinara and chipotle with sauce. Toss meatballs with sauce and bring to simmer, then spoon over rice and sprinkle with cilantro. Serve with lime wedges.

PER SERVING: About 485 calories, 10 g fat (3 g saturated), 26 g protein, 985 mg sodium, 70 g carbohydrates, 11 g fiber

TRY THIS
- Use ground turkey, pork or lamb in place of the beef.
- Serve with a noodle or grain bowl instead of over rice.
- Make Mexican meatball subs by serving the cooked meatballs in split sandwich rolls.

Mustard-Crusted Mini Meatloaves

ACTIVE TIME: 20 MINUTES ✕ TOTAL TIME: 50 MINUTES ✕ MAKES 4 SERVINGS

INGREDIENTS

- 1¼ pounds ground meat (beef or dark-meat turkey)
- 1 small zucchini, grated
- ⅓ cup seasoned breadcrumbs
- ½ teaspoon salt
- ½ teaspoon pepper
- 2 tablespoons Dijon mustard
- 3 small Gala or Empire apples, each cored and cut into 8 wedges
- 1 teaspoon fresh rosemary, chopped
- ¼ teaspoon cayenne
- 1 tablespoon extra virgin olive oil
- Snipped chives, for topping

DIRECTIONS

1. Heat oven to 425°F. In large bowl, combine ground meat, zucchini, breadcrumbs, salt and pepper. Form into 4 meatloaves and place on foil-lined rimmed baking sheet; brush with Dijon.

2. Toss apple wedges, rosemary, cayenne, oil and pinch salt; arrange around meatloaves. Bake for 30 minutes or until loaves are cooked through (165°F on an instant-read thermometer). Garnish with chives.

PER SERVING: About 420 calories, 20 g fat (7 g saturated), 32 g protein, 665 mg sodium, 24 g carbohydrates, 4 g fiber

BIG BATCH Meatloaf can be frozen for up to three months. Double or triple this recipe (loaves only; omit the apple garnish) so you'll always have some in the freezer to heat up for a cozy meal, or slice cold into a sandwich.

MAKE AHEAD

Assemble the salad the day
before and refrigerate it, covered.
Leave out the mint, cilantro,
sesame seeds and scallions, and
fold them in just before serving.

Asian Steak Noodle Bowl

INGREDIENTS

- 8 ounces buckwheat soba noodles
- 1 pound sirloin steak
- ¾ teaspoon salt, divided
- ¼ teaspoon pepper
- 1 tablespoon extra virgin olive oil
- 2 tablespoons rice vinegar
- 2 teaspoons sesame oil
- 1 teaspoon chile paste
- 1 cup spiralized carrots
- 1 cup frozen shelled edamame, thawed
- ½ cup mint leaves
- ½ cup cilantro leaves
- Toasted sesame seeds and sliced scallions, for topping

DIRECTIONS

1. Cook buckwheat soba noodles per package directions. Rinse with cold water; refrigerate.

2. Meanwhile, pat sirloin steak dry and season with ¼ teaspoon each salt and pepper. Heat large skillet on medium-high. Add olive oil, then steak, and cook to desired doneness, 5 to 7 minutes per side for medium. Let rest at least 5 minutes before slicing.

3. In large bowl, whisk together rice vinegar, sesame oil, chile paste and ½ teaspoon salt. Add soba noodles and spiralized carrots (thawed if frozen) and toss to coat. Fold in edamame, mint and cilantro leaves. Top with sliced steak, toasted sesame seeds and sliced scallions.

PER SERVING: About 545 calories, 22 g fat (7 g saturated), 37 g protein, 540 mg sodium, 53 g carbohydrates, 3 g fiber

SAME INGREDIENTS, NEW MEAL!

The reserved roasted peppers from this recipe make a quick and easy pasta sauce. Place the reserved peppers, ⅓ cup heavy cream and ¼ cup finely grated Parmesan in a blender and puree until smooth. Toss with your favorite cooked pasta, adding a bit of the pasta cooking water for a thinner sauce. Garnish with basil, more Parmesan or lemon wedges.

Fennel Roasted Chicken and Peppers

ACTIVE TIME: 20 MINUTES ✕ TOTAL TIME: 45 MINUTES ✕ MAKES 4 SERVINGS, PLUS EXTRA ROASTED PEPPERS

INGREDIENTS

- 1 tablespoon fennel seeds
- 1 tablespoon finely grated orange zest
- 6 bell peppers (red, yellow and orange), cut into 1-inch chunks
- 6 cloves garlic, thinly sliced
- 5 tablespoons extra virgin olive oil, divided
- ¾ teaspoon salt
- ¾ teaspoon pepper
- 4 small chicken legs (about 2 pounds)
- 4 cups baby spinach
- 2 ounces feta cheese, crumbled

DIRECTIONS

1. Heat oven to 425°F. In small skillet on medium heat, toast fennel seeds and orange zest until lightly browned and fragrant, 3 to 4 minutes. Transfer to spice grinder or blender and pulse to blend and grind. Set aside.

2. On large rimmed baking sheet, toss bell peppers and garlic with 4 tablespoons oil, salt and pepper. Transfer half the vegetable mixture to a second sheet and arrange everything in even layers on both sheets.

3. Rub chicken legs with remaining tablespoon oil, then with fennel-orange mixture. Nestle among vegetables on one baking sheet and roast both sheets until chicken is golden brown and cooked through and peppers are tender, 25 to 30 minutes. Set aside sheet with only vegetables (see Same Ingredients, New Meal!, opposite page); refrigerate if not using right away.

4. Transfer chicken to plates, scatter spinach over peppers and toss until just beginning to wilt. Sprinkle with feta and serve with chicken.

PER SERVING: About 470 calories, 35 g fat (11 g saturated), 32 g protein, 460 mg sodium, 9 g carbohydrates, 2 g fiber

Roast Chicken

A whole roast chicken has something for everyone—dark meat, white meat, crispy wings and a wishbone to fight over. And if you don't eat the whole bird in one sitting, remaining chicken can be pulled off the bones and used to top salads or grain bowls or fill tacos, and be tucked into enchiladas and casseroles.

BEST-EVER ROAST CHICKEN

1. Remove **4-pound chicken** from fridge at least 30 minutes before you start to cook. Heat oven to 425°F. Pat chicken dry with paper towels (do not rinse chicken).

2. With fingertips, gently separate skin from meat on chicken breast. Rub desired seasonings on meat under skin. Tie legs together with string, and rub chicken all over with **¾ teaspoon salt** (and, if desired, **1¼ teaspoons pepper**).

3. Place chicken, breast up, on a rack set inside a small roasting pan. Pour **¼ cup water** into the pan. Roast chicken 1 hour, or until juices run clear when the thickest part of the thigh is pierced with a knife (or an instant-read thermometer shows an internal temp of 165°F).

4. Lift and tilt chicken so juices inside the cavity run into the pan. Transfer chicken to a platter, and let rest 10 minutes. Meanwhile, skim and discard any fat from the pan juices. Add **¼ cup water** to the roasting pan and set it over a burner. Cook 1 minute on medium, stirring constantly.

5. Carve chicken and serve with pan juices.

FIVE ROAST CHICKEN RUBS

1 ITALIAN HERB

Mix together **1 tablespoon extra virgin olive oil or melted butter, ½ teaspoon dried basil, ½ teaspoon dried oregano, ½ teaspoon dried rosemary** and **1 clove garlic, minced.** Rub on breast meat before roasting.

2 LEMON PEPPER

Mix together **1 tablespoon extra virgin olive oil or melted butter, 2 teaspoons grated lemon peel** and **¼ teaspoon pepper.** Rub on breast meat before roasting.

3 MISO-SOY

Mix together **1 tablespoon extra virgin olive oil or melted butter, 1 teaspoon white miso** and **½ teaspoon soy sauce.** Rub on breast meat before roasting.

4 MOROCCAN

Mix together **1 tablespoon extra virgin olive oil or melted butter, ½ teaspoon ground cumin, ½ teaspoon curry powder** and **¼ teaspoon ground cinnamon.** Rub on breast meat before roasting.

5 PAPRIKA

Mix together **1 tablespoon extra virgin olive oil or melted butter, 1 teaspoon paprika** (sweet or smoked) and **½ teaspoon dried oregano.** Rub on breast meat before roasting.

Lemon-Thyme Butterflied Roast Chicken

ACTIVE TIME: 15 MINUTES ✕ **TOTAL TIME: 1 HOUR** ✕ **MAKES 4 SERVINGS**

INGREDIENTS

- 2 heads garlic, halved through equators
- 2 lemons, 1 sliced and 1 cut into wedges, divided
- 2 tablespoons olive oil, divided
- ½ bunch fresh thyme, divided
- 1 3½- to 4-pound chicken, backbone removed
- ½ teaspoon salt
- ½ teaspoon pepper

DIRECTIONS

1. Heat oven to 425°F. On large rimmed baking sheet, toss garlic halves and sliced lemon with 1 tablespoon oil and half the thyme; arrange in center of sheet. Place chicken on top, rub with remaining 1 tablespoon oil and season with salt and pepper. Scatter lemon wedges around it and roast for 20 minutes.

2. Scatter remaining thyme around chicken and roast until chicken is golden brown and cooked through (165°F on an instant-read thermometer inserted into thickest part of thigh), about 30 minutes more.

PER SERVING: About 475 calories, 27 g fat (7 g saturated), 49 g protein, 385 mg sodium, 6 g carbohydrates, 0.6 g fiber

Roasted Jerk Chicken

ACTIVE TIME: 20 MINUTES ✖ **TOTAL TIME: 1 HOUR 40 MINUTES** ✖ **MAKES 8 SERVINGS**

INGREDIENTS

- 4 scallions, sliced
- 3 cloves garlic
- 2 jalapeños, sliced
- ¼ cup canola oil
- 3 tablespoons fresh lime juice
- 3 tablespoons soy sauce
- 2 tablespoons brown sugar
- 1 teaspoon salt
- ½ teaspoon pepper
- ½ teaspoon ground allspice
- 2 whole chickens (about 4 pounds each)

DIRECTIONS

1. Heat oven to 425°F. Line large rimmed baking sheet with foil; place a roasting rack on foil.

2. In blender or food processor, blend scallions, garlic, jalapeños, oil, lime juice, soy sauce, brown sugar, salt, pepper and allspice until smooth.

3. Arrange chickens on the rack. With your hands, gently loosen the chicken skin from the meat. Spoon some scallion mixture into each chicken's cavity and under the skin; rub remaining mixture all over the outside of chicken. Tuck the wings behind each breast and tie the drumsticks together with butcher's twine. Roast 1 hour.

4. Reduce oven temperature to 375°F. Roast another 15 minutes or until chicken is cooked (165°F on an instant-read thermometer).

PER SERVING: About 600 calories, 36 g fat (9 g saturated), 60 g protein, 635 mg sodium, 5 g carbohydrates, 0.4 g fiber

SAME INGREDIENTS, NEW MEAL! If you're serving only four, eat one chicken tonight, and use the other one for Spicy Bánh Mì Sandwiches (page 147).

Plum Tomato and Eggplant Shakshuka

ACTIVE TIME: 25 MINUTES ✕ **TOTAL TIME: 1 HOUR 25 MINUTES** ✕ **MAKES 4 SERVINGS**

INGREDIENTS

- 2 eggplants (about 2 pounds total), trimmed and sliced into ¾-inch-thick rounds
- 3½ tablespoons extra virgin olive oil, divided
- ¾ teaspoon salt, divided
- ¼ cup chopped mint, divided
- 1 white onion, coarsely chopped
- 3 cloves garlic, sliced
- 2 teaspoons hot paprika
- 1 teaspoon ground cumin
- ¼ teaspoon crushed red pepper
- 5 ripe tomatoes (about 1¾ pounds), chopped, juices reserved
- ½ cup tomato puree
- ¼ teaspoon pepper
- 4 large eggs
- 2 ounces (½ cup) feta cheese, crumbled
- 2 whole-wheat pitas, toasted and halved (optional)

*without pita

DIRECTIONS

1. Heat oven to 375°F. On rimmed baking sheet, brush the eggplant with 1½ tablespoons oil and season with ¼ teaspoon salt. Roast until soft and golden, turning over once halfway, about 25 minutes. Once cool, coarsely chop the roasted eggplant and toss with 2 tablespoons mint.

2. Reset oven temperature to 425°F. Heat the remaining 2 tablespoons oil in large ovenproof skillet on medium. Add onion and garlic; cook, stirring, until they begin to brown on the edges, about 8 minutes.

3. Stir in paprika, cumin and red pepper. Cook, stirring, 1 minute. Add tomatoes, their juices and the puree; cook until tomatoes break down, stirring occasionally, about 15 minutes. Add eggplant and cook 2 minutes. Stir in pepper and remaining ½ teaspoon salt.

4. Remove from heat. With a spoon, create four indentations in the sauce, then crack in eggs. Transfer pan to oven. Cook until egg whites are set but yolks are still runny, 5 to 7 minutes. Top with feta and remaining 2 tablespoons mint. Serve with pita, if desired.

PER SERVING: About 365 calories, 21 g fat (6 g saturated), 14 g protein, 645 mg sodium, 35 g carbohydrates, 12 g fiber

Spicy Bánh Mì Sandwiches

ACTIVE TIME: 5 MINUTES ✕ **TOTAL TIME: 5 MINUTES** ✕ **MAKES 6 SERVINGS**

INGREDIENTS

- 1 Roasted Jerk Chicken (page 145)
- 1 cup mayonnaise
- 6 sandwich rolls, split and lightly toasted
- 1 Kirby cucumber, thinly sliced
- ¾ cup grated carrots
- ½ cup fresh cilantro leaves
- Sriracha hot sauce, to taste

DIRECTIONS

1. Cut meat from Roasted Jerk Chicken, discarding skin and bones; thinly slice.

2. Spread mayonnaise on rolls; top with chicken, cucumber, carrots and cilantro. Drizzle with sriracha if desired.

PER SERVING: About 610 calories, 41 g fat (7 g saturated), 34 g protein, 680 mg sodium, 25 g carbohydrates, 2 g fiber

PACK IT UP This is a great take-to-work lunch meal. Prep the night before: Shred or slice the chicken, and cut the cucumber, carrots and cilantro. Layer the vegetables and chicken in a container with a lid, and store in the refrigerator overnight. Pack the mayonnaise, hot sauce and rolls separately, and assemble sandwich at lunchtime.

Pan-Fried Chicken with Lemony Roasted Broccoli

ACTIVE TIME: 30 MINUTES ⁙ **TOTAL TIME: 30 MINUTES** ⁙ **MAKES 4 SERVINGS**

INGREDIENTS

- 1½ pounds broccoli, cut into florets
- 2 cloves garlic, thinly sliced
- 3 tablespoons extra virgin olive oil, divided
- ½ teaspoon salt, divided
- ½ teaspoon pepper, divided
- 4 6-ounce boneless, skinless chicken breasts
- 1 cup all-purpose flour
- 1 lemon, cut into ½-inch pieces
- 2 tablespoons fresh lemon juice

DIRECTIONS

1. Heat oven to 425°F. On rimmed baking sheet, toss broccoli and garlic with 1 tablespoon oil and ¼ teaspoon each salt and pepper; roast 10 minutes.

2. Meanwhile, pound chicken breasts to even thickness, season with the remaining ¼ teaspoon each salt and pepper, then coat in flour. Heat 1 tablespoon oil in large skillet on medium-high and cook chicken until golden brown, 3 to 5 minutes per side. Nestle chicken with the broccoli and roast until chicken is cooked through and broccoli is golden brown and tender, about 6 minutes.

3. Return skillet to medium heat; add remaining 1 tablespoon oil, then lemon pieces, and cook, stirring, until beginning to brown, 3 minutes. Add lemon juice and ⅓ cup water and cook, stirring and scraping up any browned bits. Spoon over chicken and serve with broccoli.

PER SERVING: About 365 calories, 15.5 g fat (2.5 g saturated), 44 g protein, 375 mg sodium, 15 g carbohydrates, 5 g fiber

MAKE AHEAD Prep the broccoli and lemons and store for up to two days before cooking. You can even buy extra broccoli and prep it to use later in the Sausage and Broccoli Quinoa Bowl (page 117).

SAME INGREDIENTS, NEW MEAL!

Buy an extra couple of chicken cutlets and use them for Creamy Lemon Pasta with Chicken and Peas (page 153). Or make more quinoa and whip up some Grain Bowls (page 180).

Chicken Quinoa Bowl

ACTIVE TIME: 15 MINUTES ✕ TOTAL TIME: 20 MINUTES ✕ MAKES 4 SERVINGS

INGREDIENTS

- 1 cup red quinoa
- 4 5-ounce boneless, skinless chicken breast cutlets
- ¼ teaspoon herbes de Provence
- ½ teaspoon salt, divided
- ¼ teaspoon pepper
- ¼ cup champagne vinegar
- ¼ cup extra virgin olive oil
- 2 scallions
- 2 tablespoons Dijon mustard
- 4 cups packed arugula
- ⅔ cup pitted green olives, quartered
- 12 ounces grape tomatoes, halved

DIRECTIONS

1. Cook quinoa per package directions.

2. Heat grill to medium-high. Season chicken breast cutlets with herbes de Provence, ¼ teaspoon salt and pepper. Grill 3 minutes per side or until cooked through.

3. In blender, puree the champagne vinegar, olive oil, scallions, mustard and remaining ¼ teaspoon salt. Toss half of vinaigrette with cooked quinoa, arugula, olives and tomatoes. Serve chicken over quinoa with remaining vinaigrette.

PER SERVING: About 500 calories, 23 g fat (4 g saturated), 36 g protein, 865 mg sodium, 35 g carbohydrates, 8 g fiber

Creamy Lemon Pasta with Chicken and Peas

ACTIVE TIME: 20 MINUTES ✕ **TOTAL TIME: 25 MINUTES** ✕ **MAKES 4 SERVINGS**

INGREDIENTS

- 2 tablespoons extra virgin olive oil
- 12 ounces boneless, skinless chicken breasts, cut into 2-inch pieces
- ¼ teaspoon salt
- ¼ teaspoon pepper
- ¼ cup fresh lemon juice
- 4 cups low-sodium chicken broth
- 12 ounces gemelli or other short pasta
- 4 ounces cream cheese, at room temp
- 1 cup peas, thawed if frozen
- 2 teaspoons finely grated lemon zest
- ½ cup finely grated Parmesan
- 1 tablespoon finely chopped tarragon

DIRECTIONS

1. Heat oil in large deep skillet on medium-high. Season chicken with salt and pepper and cook until golden brown on all sides, 4 to 5 minutes; transfer to large bowl. Add lemon juice to pan, scraping up brown bits, then pour liquid over chicken in bowl.

2. Add broth and pasta to skillet and bring to a boil. Reduce heat and simmer, stirring often, 10 minutes.

3. Return chicken (and any juices) to skillet and continue to cook until pasta is just tender, about 3 minutes.

4. Add cream cheese, stirring to melt, then fold in peas, lemon zest, Parmesan and tarragon.

PER SERVING: About 675 calories, 23.5 g fat (9 g saturated), 41 g protein, 535 mg sodium, 75 g carbohydrates, 5 g fiber

TRY THIS

If you only have boneless, skinless chicken thighs on hand (or prefer them), they're a fine substitute for chicken breasts in this recipe.

Chicken Curry

INGREDIENTS

2 tablespoons extra virgin olive oil

1 large onion, diced

6 cloves garlic, crushed with press

1 red chile, finely chopped

2 tablespoons finely grated peeled fresh ginger

1 tablespoon garam masala

1 tablespoon ground coriander

2 teaspoons sweet paprika

1 teaspoon salt, divided

2 tablespoons tomato paste

1½ pounds boneless, skinless chicken breasts, cut into 2-inch chunks

½ teaspoon pepper

1 cup low-sodium chicken broth

¼ cup plain full-fat yogurt, plus more for serving

Cooked rice and chopped cilantro, for serving

DIRECTIONS

1. Heat oil in large Dutch oven on medium-high. Add onion and cook, stirring occasionally, until it begins to change color.

2. Reduce heat to medium and cook, stirring occasionally, until tender, 3 to 4 minutes more. Stir in garlic and chile and cook 1 minute.

3. Stir in ginger, garam masala, coriander, paprika and ½ teaspoon salt and cook, stirring, 2 minutes. Stir in tomato paste and cook 2 minutes.

4. Season chicken with pepper and remaining ½ teaspoon salt, then add to pot and cook, tossing occasionally, until no longer pink, 5 minutes.

5. Stir in chicken broth and gently simmer, covered, until chicken is cooked through, 6 to 8 minutes. Stir in yogurt and heat through; serve over rice, sprinkled with cilantro.

PER SERVING: About 220 calories, 8.5 g fat (1.5 g saturated), 28 g protein, 395 mg sodium, 8 g carbohydrates, 2 g fiber

MAKE AHEAD

Stuff the chicken breasts up to
a day ahead (steps 1 and 2), and
then cover and refrigerate them
until you're ready to cook.

Cheesy Tex-Mex Stuffed Chicken

ACTIVE TIME: 30 MINUTES ✕ **TOTAL TIME: 30 MINUTES** ✕ **MAKES 4 SERVINGS**

INGREDIENTS

- 2 scallions, thinly sliced
- 2 seeded jalapeños, thinly sliced
- 1¼ cups cilantro, divided
- 1 teaspoon lime zest
- 4 ounces Monterey Jack cheese, grated
- 4 6-ounce boneless, skinless chicken breasts
- 3 tablespoons extra virgin olive oil, divided
- ½ teaspoon salt, plus more for seasoning
- Pepper
- 3 tablespoons fresh lime juice
- 2 bell peppers, thinly sliced
- ½ small red onion, thinly sliced
- 5 cups torn romaine lettuce
- Lime wedges, for serving

DIRECTIONS

1. Heat oven to 450°F. In medium bowl, combine scallions and jalapeños, ¼ cup chopped cilantro, and lime zest, then toss with Monterey Jack cheese. Set aside.

2. Insert knife into thickest part of each chicken breast and move back and forth to create a 2½-inch pocket that is as wide as possible without going through. Stuff chicken with cheese mixture.

3. Heat 2 tablespoons oil in large skillet on medium. Season chicken with salt and pepper and cook until golden brown on one side, 3 to 4 minutes. Turn chicken over and roast until cooked through, 10 to 12 minutes.

4. Meanwhile, in large bowl, whisk together lime juice, remaining 1 tablespoon oil and ½ teaspoon salt. Add bell peppers and red onion and let sit 10 minutes, tossing occasionally. Toss with romaine lettuce and remaining 1 cup cilantro. Serve with chicken and lime wedges.

PER SERVING: About 360 calories, 22 g fat (7.5 g saturated), 32 g protein, 715 mg sodium, 10 g carbohydrates, 3 g fiber

Enchiladas Verdes

ACTIVE TIME: 25 MINUTES ✂ **TOTAL TIME: 25 MINUTES** ✂ **MAKES 4 SERVINGS**

INGREDIENTS

For the salsa verde

½   pound tomatillos (about 4), husked, rinsed and halved

2   cloves unpeeled garlic

1   large onion, cut into 1-inch-thick wedges

1   large poblano pepper, halved and seeded

1   jalapeño, halved and seeded

1   tablespoon extra virgin olive oil

1   teaspoon salt, divided

½   teaspoon pepper

3   tablespoons fresh lime juice

3   cups fresh cilantro

For the enchiladas

3   cups shredded rotisserie chicken

2   scallions, thinly sliced

4   tablespoons fresh lime juice, divided

1   cup fresh cilantro, divided

1½   cups Monterey Jack cheese, grated, divided

8   corn tortillas

1   small red onion, thinly sliced

DIRECTIONS

1. Heat broiler. On large rimmed baking sheet, toss tomatillos, garlic, onion, poblano and jalapeño with oil, ½ teaspoon salt and pepper. Turn peppers cut side down and broil, rotating pan every 5 minutes until the vegetables are tender and charred, about 15 minutes. Reduce temp to 425°F.

2. When cool enough to handle, discard skins from poblano and garlic and transfer all vegetables to blender. Add lime juice, cilantro, and remaining ½ teaspoon salt and puree until smooth. Set salsa verde aside.

3. To prepare enchiladas, in large bowl, toss chicken with scallions and 2 tablespoons lime juice. Fold in ½ cup cilantro and 1 cup cheese.

4. Spread ½ cup salsa in a 9- by 13-inch baking dish and transfer the rest to a bowl. Working with one tortilla at a time, dip it in salsa, then fill it with about ½ cup chicken mixture. Roll the chicken mixture in the tortilla and place it seam side down in the dish. Repeat.

5. Top with remaining salsa and ½ cup cheese. Bake until beginning to brown, 8 to 10 minutes.

6. Meanwhile, in small bowl, toss red onion, remaining 2 tablespoons lime juice, and pinch each salt and pepper. Serve over enchiladas and top with remaining cilantro, if desired.

PER SERVING: About 500 calories, 32 g fat (11 g saturated), 30 g protein, 1,215 mg sodium, 39 g carbohydrates, 6 g fiber

Seared Coconut-Lime Chicken with Snap Pea Slaw

ACTIVE TIME: 35 MINUTES ✕ **TOTAL TIME: 35 MINUTES** ✕ **MAKES 4 SERVINGS**

INGREDIENTS

- 2 tablespoons toasted sesame oil
- 1 tablespoon grated peeled fresh ginger
- 3 tablespoons fresh lime juice, divided
- 1 teaspoon salt, divided
- 10 ounces snap peas, strings removed and thinly sliced
- 4 ounces snow peas, thinly sliced
- 2 scallions, thinly sliced
- 2 8-ounce boneless, skinless chicken breasts
- 1 tablespoon extra virgin olive oil
- ½ teaspoon pepper
- 2 tablespoons coconut cream
- ½ cup cilantro

DIRECTIONS

1. In large bowl, whisk together sesame oil, ginger, 1½ tablespoons lime juice and ½ teaspoon salt. Add snap peas, snow peas and scallions, and toss to combine. Set aside.

2. Cut each chicken breast horizontally in half to make 4 thin cutlets, then pound to ¼-inch thickness. Heat olive oil in large skillet on medium-high. Season chicken with pepper and remaining ½ teaspoon salt and cook in batches until golden brown and cooked through, about 2 minutes per side. Transfer chicken to plates as it is cooked.

3. Remove pan from heat and stir in coconut cream and remaining 1½ tablespoons lime juice, scraping up any browned bits. Spoon over chicken on plates.

4. Fold cilantro into pea mixture and serve on top of chicken.

PER SERVING: About 290 calories, 15 g fat (3.5 g saturated), 29 g protein, 540 mg sodium, 10 g carbohydrates, 3 g fiber

TRY THIS Make extra lime-sesame dressing and drizzle it over a grain or noodle bowl.

TRY THIS

Serve kebabs over another grain of
your choice — rice, quinoa, etc. — or
with a green salad instead of a grain.

Grilled Chicken Kebabs

ACTIVE TIME: 20 MINUTES ✖ **TOTAL TIME: 20 MINUTES** ✖ **MAKES 4 SERVINGS**

INGREDIENTS

- 1 cup quick-cooking bulgur
- ¼ cup harissa
- 2 tablespoons extra virgin olive oil
- 2 tablespoons honey
- 1¼ pounds boneless, skinless chicken breasts, thinly sliced
- 1 15-ounce can chickpeas, rinsed
- ¾ cup finely chopped fresh parsley
- ½ teaspoon salt

DIRECTIONS

1. Prepare bulgur per package directions. In large bowl, whisk harissa with oil and honey; set half aside for serving.

2. Heat grill to medium-high. Toss sliced chicken breasts in remaining harissa mixture, then thread onto skewers. Grill 6 minutes or until cooked through, turning over once.

3. Toss chickpeas with bulgur, parsley and salt. Serve chicken on top with reserved harissa sauce.

PER SERVING: About 495 calories, 13 g fat (2 g saturated), 39 g protein, 560 mg sodium, 57 g carbohydrates, 13 g fiber

Sheet-Pan Chickpea Chicken

ACTIVE TIME: 5 MINUTES ✕ **TOTAL TIME: 30 MINUTES** ✕ **MAKES 4 SERVINGS**

INGREDIENTS

- 1 15-ounce can chickpeas, rinsed
- 1 16-ounce bag mini sweet peppers
- 2 tablespoons olive oil, divided
- ¼ teaspoon salt
- ¼ teaspoon pepper
- 2 tablespoons harissa
- 4 small skin-on chicken legs (about 2½ pounds)

Chopped cilantro, for serving

DIRECTIONS

1. Heat oven to 425°F. On large rimmed baking sheet, toss chickpeas and peppers with 1 tablespoon oil, salt and pepper.

2. In small bowl, whisk together harissa and remaining 1 tablespoon oil. Rub chicken with harissa mixture, and then nestle among chickpeas and peppers. Roast until chicken is golden brown and cooked through, 20 to 25 minutes.

3. Toss with cilantro before serving.

PER SERVING: About 630 calories, 42 g fat (10 g saturated), 39 g protein, 600 mg sodium, 22 g carbohydrates, 6 g fiber

TEST KITCHEN TIP Sheet-pan meals are a quick and easy way to get dinner on the table in minutes. Try some of these other combinations:
- Italian sausage, apples and sliced cabbage
- Salmon fillets and halved Brussels sprouts
- Sheet-pan nachos: Layer chips with cooked ground beef, pinto beans and grated cheese. Bake until cheese melts and then top with diced avocado and salsa.

Curried Chicken Salad Wraps

ACTIVE TIME: 10 MINUTES ⁙ **TOTAL TIME: 10 MINUTES** ⁙ **MAKES 4 SERVINGS**

INGREDIENTS

- ¼ cup mayonnaise
- 2 tablespoons plain Greek yogurt
- 1 tablespoon fresh lemon juice
- 1¼ teaspoons curry powder
- ½ teaspoon Dijon mustard
- 1 stalk celery, finely chopped
- 2 scallions, thinly sliced
- 3 cups shredded white meat from rotisserie chicken
- ¼ cup golden raisins
- ¼ cup toasted chopped almonds
- 2 cups mixed greens
- 4 10-inch wraps

DIRECTIONS

1. In medium bowl, whisk together mayonnaise, yogurt, lemon juice, curry powder, mustard, celery and scallions. Fold in chicken, raisins and almonds.

2. Divide greens evenly among wraps, top with chicken salad and roll tightly.

PER SERVING: About 540 calories, 23 g fat (5 g saturated), 39 g protein, 1,035 mg sodium, 47 g carbohydrates, 6 g fiber

MAKE AHEAD Make the chicken salad up to 2 days ahead of time and store in the refrigerator. Get out the greens and wraps at lunchtime and assemble.

TRY THIS While you can easily use flour tortillas for the wraps, any carrier will work—spinach wraps, large lettuce or kale leaves, or even sandwich rolls or bread.

Avocado and Tuna Salad Wraps

ACTIVE TIME: 10 MINUTES ❋ **TOTAL TIME: 10 MINUTES** ❋ **MAKES 4 SERVINGS**

INGREDIENTS

1½ tablespoons extra virgin olive oil

1 tablespoon fresh lemon juice

½ teaspoon salt

½ teaspoon pepper

2 5-ounce cans solid white tuna in water, rinsed

1 avocado, cut into chunks

2 scallions, thinly sliced

2 cups mixed greens

4 10-inch wraps

DIRECTIONS

1. In a medium bowl, whisk together oil, lemon juice, salt and pepper. Toss with tuna, avocado and scallions.

2. Divide greens among wraps, top with tuna salad and roll tightly.

PER SERVING: About 415 calories, 18 g fat (4 g saturated), 24 g protein, 1,050 mg sodium, 41 g carbohydrates, 8 g fiber

PACK IT UP Mix the tuna and scallions with the lemon juice, oil, and salt and pepper up to a day before, and store in the fridge. At lunchtime, cut up avocado and add it to the tuna, and then assemble the wraps.

Sheet-Pan Shrimp and Zoodles

ACTIVE TIME: 10 MINUTES ✢ **TOTAL TIME: 25 MINUTES** ✢ **MAKES 4 SERVINGS**

INGREDIENTS

1½ pounds medium zucchini (about 4), spiralized

2 tablespoons extra virgin olive oil, divided

½ teaspooon salt, divided

½ teaspoon pepper, divided

20 large peeled and deveined shrimp

4 scallions, thinly sliced

4 cloves garlic, thinly sliced

1 small red chile, thinly sliced

2 tablespoons dry white wine

1 tablespoon fresh lemon juice

4 ounces feta cheese, crumbled

DIRECTIONS

1. Heat oven to 475°F. On large rimmed baking sheet, toss zucchini with 1 tablespoon oil and ¼ teaspoon each salt and pepper; arrange in an even layer and roast 6 minutes.

2. Meanwhile, in large bowl, toss shrimp, scallions, garlic and chile with wine, lemon juice and remaining ¼ teaspoon each salt and pepper.

3. Scatter shrimp over zucchini and drizzle with remaining 1 tablespoon oil, then sprinkle with feta. Roast until shrimp are opaque throughout, 5 to 7 minutes.

PER SERVING: About 200 calories, 13.5 g fat (5.5 g saturated), 11 g protein, 715 mg sodium, 10 g carbohydrates, 2 g fiber

No-Cook Shrimp Rolls

ACTIVE TIME: 15 MINUTES ✳ TOTAL TIME: 15 MINUTES ✳ MAKES 4 SANDWICHES

INGREDIENTS

- 4 small radishes, thinly sliced
- 2 scallions, thinly sliced into matchsticks
- 1 small carrot, peeled into ribbons
- ¼ cup fresh lime juice, divided
- ¼ cup fresh mint leaves
- 3 tablespoons mayonnaise
- 1 tablespoon gochujang
- 1¼ pounds peeled cooked shrimp
- 4 sandwich rolls, split

DIRECTIONS

1. In medium bowl, toss radishes, scallions and carrot with 2 tablespoons lime juice; fold in mint leaves.

2. In large bowl, whisk together mayonnaise, remaining 2 tablespoons lime juice and gochujang. Cut shrimp into bite-size pieces and toss with sauce. Fill buns with shrimp mixture and top with carrot ribbon salad.

PER SERVING: About 375 calories, 14.5 g fat (2.5 g saturated), 30 g protein, 1,525 mg sodium, 30 g carbohydrates, 2 g fiber

TEST KITCHEN TIP Turn these sammies into a salad. Omit the bread and toss this mixture with one 5-ounce package of your favorite mixed greens.

TRY THIS

Shirataki noodles are made from a
Japanese yam, and they are almost
entirely calorie- and carb-free. But
if you can't find them, try another
veggie noodle, like zucchini noodles.

Peanutty Edamame and Noodle Bowl

ACTIVE TIME: 20 MINUTES ✕ **TOTAL TIME: 20 MINUTES** ✕ **MAKES 4 SERVINGS**

INGREDIENTS

- 3   8-ounce bags shirataki noodles, rinsed and drained
- 3   cups frozen shelled edamame
- 2   cups frozen corn
- ½   cup peanut butter
- ½   cup rice vinegar
- 2   tablespoons water
- 1   tablespoon sriracha hot sauce, plus more for serving
- ½   teaspoon salt
- 3   cups grated carrots
- 1   pint grape tomatoes, halved
- 1   medium Granny Smith apple, cored and thinly sliced
- ½   cup fresh cilantro, chopped

DIRECTIONS

1. Fill large saucepot with water and bring to a boil. Add shirataki noodles, edamame and corn; boil 2 minutes. Drain, rinse and drain again.

2. In large bowl, whisk peanut butter, vinegar, water, sriracha and salt. Add carrots, tomatoes, apple, cilantro and noodle mixture. Toss until well coated. Serve with sriracha.

PER SERVING: About 455 calories, 22 g fat (3 g saturated), 22 g protein, 540 mg sodium, 50 g carbohydrates, 13 g fiber

SAME INGREDIENTS, NEW MEAL!

Buy extra cashews and turn what you don't use for this recipe into Sweet and Spicy Nuts (page 204).

Crispy Tofu Bowl

ACTIVE TIME: 20 MINUTES ✕ **TOTAL TIME: 30 MINUTES** ✕ **MAKES 4 SERVINGS**

INGREDIENTS

1 cup quinoa

14 ounces extra-firm tofu

½ small red onion, very thinly sliced

¼ cup red wine vinegar

¼ cup Thai sweet chile sauce

1 tablespoon extra virgin olive oil

¼ teaspoon salt

1 English cucumber, chopped

3 tablespoons cornstarch

2 tablespoons vegetable oil

2 tablespoons roasted cashew halves

Parsley leaves, for topping

DIRECTIONS

1. Cook quinoa per package directions.

2. Slice tofu into ¼-inch-thick pieces. Place on a cutting board between paper towels; top with a baking sheet. Place large cans or other weight on top of the baking sheet, and then let stand 10 minutes. In small bowl, soak red onion in cold water.

3. Whisk vinegar and chile sauce with olive oil and salt. Drain onion, pat dry and toss with cucumber and half the vinaigrette.

4. Sprinkle cornstarch on both sides of the sliced tofu. Heat vegetable oil in a 12-inch skillet on medium-high until hot. Carefully add tofu. Cook until deep golden brown, 2 to 3 minutes per side. Drain on paper towels.

5. Divide quinoa among 4 bowls. Top each with cucumber salad, cashews, parsley and tofu. Serve with remaining vinaigrette.

PER SERVING: About 440 calories, 20 g fat (2 g saturated), 18 g protein, 310 mg sodium, 45 g carbohydrates, 5 g fiber

TEST KITCHEN TIP If you like your tofu extra crispy, let it stand 30 minutes instead of 10 minutes in step 2.

Lentil Bolognese

ACTIVE TIME: 20 MINUTES ✗ **TOTAL TIME: 40 MINUTES** ✗ **MAKES 6 SERVINGS**

INGREDIENTS

- 2 cloves garlic
- 1 small onion, chopped
- 1 medium carrot, chopped
- 6 ounces button mushrooms
- 1 tablespoon extra virgin olive oil
- ½ teaspoon dried oregano
- ¼ teaspoon red pepper flakes
- ½ teaspoon salt, divided
- ½ teaspoon pepper, divided
- 8 ounces ground beef (at least 90% lean)
- 1 tablespoon tomato paste
- 1 14-ounce can whole tomatoes
- ½ cup dried red lentils
- 1 pound spaghetti
- ⅓ cup toasted pine nuts (optional)
- Grated pecorino cheese, for serving (optional)

DIRECTIONS

1. In food processor, pulse together garlic, onion, carrot and mushrooms until finely chopped.

2. Heat oil in large skillet on medium. Add chopped vegetables, oregano, red pepper flakes and ¼ teaspoon each salt and pepper and cook, covered, stirring occasionally, until tender, 4 to 5 minutes. Add beef and cook, breaking up with wooden spoon, until browned, 10 to 12 minutes.

3. Stir in tomato paste and cook 1 minute. Add tomatoes (and their juices), crushing with your hands as you add to skillet. Add lentils, 2 cups water and remaining ¼ teaspoon each salt and pepper; simmer until lentils are tender, 15 to 20 minutes.

4. Meanwhile, cook pasta per package directions. Drain and toss with sauce. Top with pine nuts and pecorino, if desired.

PER SERVING: About 535 calories, 14 g fat (3 g saturated), 27 g protein, 380 mg sodium, 75 g carbohydrates, 10 g fiber

BIG BATCH This sauce freezes well, so consider doubling the recipe.

MAKE AHEAD

The tortillas can be filled, wrapped
and frozen up to 2 months without
the sauce. Or you can keep the whole
casserole assembled in the fridge
for up to a day before baking.

Butternut Mole Enchiladas

ACTIVE TIME: 25 MINUTES ✻ **TOTAL TIME: 1 HOUR** ✻ **MAKES 6 SERVINGS**

INGREDIENTS

For the squash

- 2 pounds butternut squash, peeled, seeded and cut into ½-inch pieces
- 1 tablespoon extra virgin olive oil
- ¼ teaspoon chile powder
- Kosher salt and pepper

For the mole sauce

- 1 15-ounce can tomato sauce
- 2 cloves garlic
- ½ small onion, chopped
- 1 chipotle in adobo, plus 1 tablespoon adobo sauce
- 1 tablespoon fresh lime juice
- ½ teaspoon ground cinnamon
- ¼ teaspoon salt
- ¼ teaspoon pepper
- ¼ cup smooth peanut butter
- 3 ounces semisweet chocolate

For the enchiladas

- 12 soft corn tortillas
- 1 15-ounce can black beans, rinsed
- 4 ounces queso fresco, crumbled, plus more for topping
- 1 avocado, cut into chunks
- Toasted pumpkin seeds and chopped cilantro (optional)

DIRECTIONS

1. Heat oven to 400°F. On large rimmed baking sheet, toss squash with oil, chile powder and a pinch each salt and pepper. Roast until tender, 15 to 20 minutes. Set aside. Lower oven temperature to 350°F.

2. Meanwhile, make the mole sauce: In blender, puree tomato sauce, garlic, onion, chipotle chile and adobo sauce, lime juice, cinnamon, salt and pepper until smooth. Transfer mixture to small saucepan and simmer on medium heat for 4 minutes. Add peanut butter and chocolate, stirring until melted and smooth. Remove from heat.

3. Coat a 9- by 13-inch baking dish with nonstick cooking spray, then spread one-third of the mole sauce on the bottom. Fill each tortilla with a scant ¼ cup squash and 1 tablespoon each black beans and queso fresco. Roll and place seam side down in prepared dish.

4. Spoon another one-third of mole over top, cover and bake 20 minutes. Uncover, spread with remaining mole and bake 5 minutes more. Remove from oven and top with avocado and queso fresco, and pumpkin seeds and cilantro, if desired.

PER SERVING: About 490 calories, 25 g fat (8 g saturated), 15 g protein, 865 mg sodium, 60 g carbohydrates, 13 g fiber

EASY AS 1, 2, 3...

Grain Bowls

How about an immensely satisfying meal that fits snugly in a single bowl? It's as simple as choosing a base, some toppings and a sauce to pull the dish together. Stack grain bowl elements from the base up.

FRIED RICE

The combinations at right make for delicious grain bowls, but you can also use them to make creative spins on fried rice (or quinoa or farro, etc.). Toss day-old grains with some protein and veggies, then fry it all up in a hot skillet or wok and finish with toppings and a drizzle of the sauce of your choice. See Vegetarian Fried Rice with Shiitakes and Edamame, page 185, for complete fried-rice directions.

IDEAS TO GET YOU STARTED

Here are some simple combinations to inspire your grain bowls.

Quinoa • Cucumbers and Tomatoes • Grilled Chicken (left over from Grilled Chicken Kebabs, page 163) • Feta • Tahini Dressing

Basmati rice • Sautéed Kale and Broccoli • Sliced Pan-Seared Steak (left over from Asian Steak Noodle Bowl, page 137) • Chopped Scallions • Teriyaki Sauce

Farro (left over from Grilled Halloumi Salad, page 109) • Kale • Chickpea Salad • Parmesan Cheese • Squeeze of Lemon

Brown Rice • Avocado and Red Cabbage • Carnitas (left over from Carnitas Tacos, page 125) • Grated Monterey Jack Cheese • Salsa Verde

Fried White Rice • Crispy Tofu (left over from Crispy Tofu Bowl, page 175) • Bok Choy • Snap Peas • Kimchi • Egg

BUILD A BOWL

Mix and match these five elements for a quick and delicious main meal.

1 BASES
Brown or White Rice • Bulgur • Farro • Polenta • Quinoa

2 VEGGIES
Bell Pepper • Bok Choy • Broccoli • Cauliflower • Chard • Cherry Tomatoes • Eggplant • Green Beans • Kale • Onion • Spinach • Winter Squash • Zucchini

3 PROTEINS
Beans • Chickpeas • Cooked Lentils • Fried Tofu • Hard-Boiled Eggs • Pulled or Shredded Pork • Sliced Grilled or Roast Chicken • Sliced Seared or Grilled Steak

4 TOPPINGS
Crumbled Feta or Goat Cheese • Pickled or Fermented Vegetables • Toasted Sesame or Sunflower Seeds • Torn or Chopped Herbs

5 SAUCES
Pesto • Salsas • Tahini Dressing • Teriyaki Sauce • Vinaigrettes

SAME INGREDIENTS, NEW MEAL!

This recipe yields enough risotto to make the Crispy Caprese Cakes (page 184). You can refrigerate the extra risotto for up to 4 days before using it.

Wild Mushroom Risotto

ACTIVE TIME: 25 MINUTES ⁘ TOTAL TIME: 40 MINUTES ⁘ MAKES 4 SERVINGS, PLUS EXTRA RISOTTO

INGREDIENTS

- 4 tablespoons extra virgin olive oil, divided
- 1 large onion, finely chopped
- 4 cloves garlic, crushed with press, divided
- 2 cups Arborio rice
- 1 cup dry white wine
- 4 cups low-sodium chicken broth or water
- ¾ teaspoon salt
- ¾ teaspoon pepper
- 1 cup finely grated Parmesan
- 1 pound mixed wild mushrooms, stemmed and sliced
- 1 red chile, thinly sliced
- 2 sprigs thyme, broken into small pieces
- 4 fried eggs, for serving (optional)

DIRECTIONS

1. Heat 2 tablespoons oil in large saucepan on medium. Add onion and cook, covered, stirring occasionally, until tender, 6 to 8 minutes. Stir in half of the garlic and cook 2 minutes. Add rice and wine and cook, stirring, until wine is absorbed, about 3 minutes.

2. Add broth (or water), salt and pepper and bring to a boil. Reduce heat and simmer, covered, until liquid is absorbed and rice is tender, 18 to 20 minutes. Stir in Parmesan. Spread 3 cups of the risotto on a parchment-lined baking sheet and let cool. Set aside or refrigerate (covered) for later use (see Same Ingredients, New Meal!, opposite page).

3. Meanwhile, heat remaining 2 tablespoons oil in large skillet on medium-high. Cook half of mushrooms, tossing occasionally, until golden brown, 6 to 8 minutes, then transfer to a plate. Repeat with the remaining mushrooms, adding chile, thyme and remaining garlic once browned, and cook 2 minutes more. Toss with the first batch of mushrooms.

4. Serve mushrooms over risotto, topped with a fried egg if desired.

PER SERVING: About 450 calories, 16.5 g fat (3.5 g saturated), 16 g protein, 470 mg sodium, 64 g carbohydrates, 5 g fiber

Crispy Caprese Cakes

ACTIVE TIME: 30 MINUTES ✂ **TOTAL TIME: 55 MINUTES** ✂ **MAKES 4 SERVINGS**

INGREDIENTS

- 1 pint grape tomatoes, halved
- 1 clove garlic, pressed
- 3 tablespoons extra virgin olive oil, divided, plus more as needed
- ¼ teaspoon salt
- ¼ teaspoon pepper
- 3 large eggs
- 1 tablespoon water
- 1½ cups panko
- 3 cups cooled Wild Mushroom Risotto (page 183), or another type of risotto
- 4 ounces fresh mozzarella, torn into bite-size pieces
- Green salad, for serving (optional)

DIRECTIONS

1. Heat oven to 300°F. On a parchment-lined rimmed baking sheet, toss tomatoes and garlic with 1 tablespoon oil, salt and pepper. Roast until beginning to break down, 20 to 30 minutes.

2. Meanwhile, in medium bowl, whisk together eggs and water. Place panko in shallow bowl. Using large cookie scoop or hands, form cooled risotto into 8 balls. With damp hands, gently form each ball into a 2-inch cake. Dip each cake into egg mixture, letting excess drip off, and then into panko, pressing gently to help it adhere.

3. Heat remaining 2 tablespoons oil in large skillet on medium. Place half the rice cakes in skillet and cook until golden brown, about 4 minutes. Using thin spatula, gently turn cakes over and cook until golden brown, 3 to 4 minutes more. Transfer cakes to plates and repeat with remaining rice cakes, adding more oil as necessary.

4. Toss tomatoes with mozzarella and serve over rice cakes with salad, if desired.

PER SERVING: About 570 calories, 28 g fat (8.5 g saturated), 23 g protein, 565 mg sodium, 61 g carbohydrates, 3 g fiber

Vegetarian Fried Rice with Shiitakes and Edamame

ACTIVE TIME: 25 MINUTES ❊ TOTAL TIME: 25 MINUTES ❊ MAKES 4 SERVINGS

INGREDIENTS

- 5 tablespoons fresh lime juice
- 2 tablespoons reduced-sodium soy sauce
- 2 teaspoons fish sauce
- 1 teaspoon sugar
- 4 tablespoons canola oil, divided
- 8 ounces tiny shiitake mushrooms (or shiitake mushroom caps), sliced
- 4 scallions, thinly sliced
- 1 1-inch piece ginger, peeled and cut into matchsticks
- 2 cloves garlic, thinly sliced
- 1 jalapeño, seeded if desired, thinly sliced
- 4 cups cooked basmati rice
- 1 cup edamame, thawed if frozen
- 4 large fried eggs

Fresh cilantro leaves, for serving (optional)

Lime wedges, for serving (optional)

DIRECTIONS

1. In small bowl, combine lime juice, soy sauce, fish sauce and sugar. Set aside.

2. Heat 2 tablespoons oil in large skillet over medium-high heat. Add mushrooms and cook, tossing until just golden brown, 2 to 3 minutes. Transfer to a plate.

3. Return skillet to medium-high heat. Add remaining 2 tablespoons oil, then scallions, ginger, garlic and jalapeño and cook, stirring for 1 minute. Add the rice and edamame and cook, tossing to combine for 1 minute.

4. Add the soy sauce mixture along with reserved mushrooms and toss to combine. Top each serving with an egg. Serve with fresh cilantro and lime wedges, if desired.

PER SERVING: About 490 calories, 24 g fat (13 g saturated), 18 g protein, 575 mg sodium, 53 g carbohydrates, 4 g fiber

TEST KITCHEN TIP To make this dish vegan, omit the fried eggs and substitute soy sauce or coconut aminos for the fish sauce.

MAKE AHEAD

Bake a batch of sweet potatoes ahead of time and store them in the fridge. They reheat beautifully and can be topped with anything — roast or rotisserie chicken, bacon crumbles and a fried egg, walnuts and blue cheese, and veggie or meat chili — for a fast and fresh weeknight dinner.

Loaded Sweet Potatoes

ACTIVE TIME: 10 MINUTES ✕ **TOTAL TIME: 35 MINUTES** ✕ **MAKES 4 SERVINGS**

INGREDIENTS

- 4 medium sweet potatoes
- 1 15-ounce can black beans, rinsed
- ¼ cup crumbled feta
- ¼ cup roasted red peppers
- 3 tablespoons extra virgin olive oil
- 3 tablespoons finely chopped parsley
- ¼ teaspoon salt

DIRECTIONS

1. Heat oven to 400°F.

2. With small knife, poke sweet potatoes all over; arrange in large baking dish. Microwave on High 10 to 12 minutes or until easily pierced with knife.

3. Line large baking sheet with foil. In medium bowl, combine black beans, feta, peppers, oil, parsley and salt. Cut lengthwise slits in the sweet potatoes. With a fork, scrape sweet potato flesh to fluff; add black bean mixture to each potato half, packing to fit, and place on prepared baking sheet. Bake for 10 minutes or until beans are hot.

PER SERVING: About 345 calories, 13 g fat (3 g saturated), 10 g protein, 525 mg sodium, 50 g carbohydrates, 13 g fiber

Speedy Eggplant Parmesan

ACTIVE TIME: 20 MINUTES ✕ **TOTAL TIME: 40 MINUTES** ✕ **MAKES 4 SERVINGS**

INGREDIENTS

- ½ cup all-purpose flour
- 1 large egg plus 1 egg white
- 1 cup panko
- ½ cup freshly grated Parmesan cheese
- ½ teaspoon garlic powder
- ½ teaspoon salt
- ¼ teaspoon pepper
- 1 tablespoon extra virgin olive oil
- 1 small eggplant (about 12 ounces)
- 1 16- to 18-ounce package cheese ravioli
- 1 cup jarred marinara sauce, warmed

Grated fresh mozzarella, for serving (optional)

DIRECTIONS

1. Heat oven to 450°F. Line large baking sheet with nonstick foil.

2. Place flour on a plate and beat egg and egg white in shallow bowl. In second shallow bowl or pie plate, combine panko, Parmesan, garlic powder, salt and pepper, and then mix with oil.

3. Cut eggplant into long ½-inch-thick sticks. Coat eggplant sticks in flour, then egg (letting any excess drip off), and then coat in panko mixture, pressing gently to help it adhere. Transfer sticks to prepared baking sheet and roast, turning halfway through, until golden brown, 15 to 18 minutes.

4. Meanwhile, cook ravioli per package instructions. Drain, divide among plates and top with sauce. Cut eggplant sticks into pieces and scatter on top of ravioli. Serve with fresh mozzarella, if desired.

PER SERVING: About 485 calories, 22 g fat (7 g saturated), 23 g protein, 1,115 mg sodium, 70 g carbohydrates, 8 g fiber

Apple Snacks with Almond Butter and Pomegranate, page 201

Snacks

Easy Yogurt Dip

ACTIVE TIME: 5 MINUTES ✕ **TOTAL TIME: 5 MINUTES** ✕ **MAKES 2 SERVINGS**

INGREDIENTS

1   7-ounce container Greek yogurt

2   tablespoons crumbled feta

1   scallion, finely chopped

1   tablespoon mint, chopped

2   teaspoons fresh lemon juice

Pepper

Vegetables, such as sliced cucumbers, snap peas and radishes, for serving

DIRECTIONS

1. In medium bowl, combine yogurt, feta, scallion, mint and lemon juice and season with pepper.

2. Place dip in a serving dish with veggies on the side for dipping. Dip will keep in refrigerator for 2 days.

PER SERVING: About 125 calories, 7 g fat (4 g saturated), 11 g protein, 125 mg sodium, 6 g carbohydrates, 0.5 g fiber

TRY THIS Drizzle this dip over a grain bowl or grilled meat.

Zucchini Tots

ACTIVE TIME: 10 MINUTES ✄ **TOTAL TIME: 30 MINUTES** ✄ **MAKES 24 TOTS / 4 SERVINGS**

INGREDIENTS

- 2 medium zucchini (about 12 ounces total)
- 1 large egg, beaten
- ½ cup grated pecorino
- ½ cup panko
- 1 clove garlic, crushed with press
- ½ teaspoon pepper

DIRECTIONS

1. Heat oven to 400°F. Coat large baking sheet with nonstick cooking spray. Grate zucchini and squeeze dry with paper towels. Mix zucchini with egg, pecorino, panko, garlic and pepper.

2. Use small cookie scoop to drop tablespoonfuls of mixture onto prepared baking sheet. Then, shape each into a small log. Bake, turning halfway through, until golden brown, 20 to 22 minutes.

PER SERVING: About 145 calories, 6 g fat (3.5 g saturated), 12 g protein, 300 mg sodium, 12 g carbohydrates, 1 g fiber

MAKE AHEAD Make these tots ahead of time and refrigerate for up to three days. Pop them in a toaster oven on a piece of foil and toast on a dark setting to re-crisp.

Chickpea "Nuts"

ACTIVE TIME: 5 MINUTES ✕ **TOTAL TIME: 35 MINUTES** ✕ **MAKES 2 CUPS / 8 SERVINGS**

INGREDIENTS

- 2 15-ounce cans chickpeas, rinsed
- 2 tablespoons extra virgin olive oil
- ¼ teaspoon salt
- ¼ teaspoon pepper

DIRECTIONS

1. Heat oven to 425°F. Pat chickpeas very dry with paper towels, discarding any loose skins.

2. On large rimmed baking sheet, toss chickpeas with oil, salt and pepper. Roast, occasionally shaking pan, for 30 minutes, until crisp. Remove from oven and transfer to bowl and toss with additional seasonings if desired. Chickpeas will continue to crisp as they cool. If not eating immediately, let cool completely then store in an airtight container for up to 1 week. To re-crisp heat at 425°F for 8 minutes.

PER SERVING: About 110 calories, 5 g fat (0.5 g saturated), 4 g protein, 180 mg sodium, 13 g carbohydrates, 4 g fiber

Flavor Your "Nuts"

HONEY-SESAME

- 2 tablespoons honey
- 1 tablespoon sesame oil
- 1 tablespoon sesame seeds
- 1 tablespoon sugar
- ½ teaspoon garlic powder
- ½ teaspoon five-spice powder

In small bowl, combine all ingredients. Follow original recipe instructions, then toss roasted chickpeas with honey mixture. Return to oven for 5 minutes until caramelized and crisp.

BBQ

- 1 teaspoon dark brown sugar
- ½ teaspoon ground cumin
- ½ teaspoon ground paprika
- ½ teaspoon garlic powder
- ½ teaspoon chile powder

In small bowl, combine all ingredients. Follow original recipe instructions, then toss roasted chickpeas in brown sugar mixture.

SPICY BUFFALO

- ¼ cup cayenne pepper hot sauce

Follow original recipe instructions, then toss roasted chickpeas with cayenne pepper hot sauce. Return to oven for 5 minutes until dry and crisp.

MASALA

- ½ teaspoon garam masala
- ½ teaspoon ground cumin
- ½ teaspoon ground ginger
- ¼ teaspoon cayenne pepper

In small bowl, combine all ingredients. Follow original recipe instructions, then toss roasted chickpeas with garam masala mixture. Return to oven for 5 minutes until dry and crisp.

MAPLE-CINNAMON

- 2 tablespoons maple syrup
- 2 teaspoons sugar
- 1 teaspoon ground cinnamon
- ¼ teaspoon ground nutmeg

In small bowl, combine all ingredients. Follow original recipe instructions, then toss roasted chickpeas in maple mixture. Return to oven for 5 minutes until caramelized and crisp.

PARMESAN-HERB

- ¼ cup finely grated Parmesan
- 1 teaspoon garlic powder
- 1 teaspoon finely chopped fresh rosemary
- 1 teaspoon finely grated, loosely packed lemon zest

In small bowl, combine all ingredients. Follow original recipe instructions, then toss roasted chickpeas in Parmesan mixture.

SAME INGREDIENT, NEW MEAL!

Pumpkin seeds add great crunch to a delicious and nutritious breakfast treat. Reserve ½ cup roasted pumpkin seeds for Pumpkin-Cherry Breakfast Cookies (page 53).

Roasted Pumpkin Seeds

ACTIVE TIME: 15 MINUTES � **TOTAL TIME: 1 HOUR 35 MINUTES** ✳ **MAKES 8 SERVINGS (2 CUPS)**

INGREDIENTS

1 medium pumpkin

2 tablespoons extra virgin olive oil

Kosher salt

DIRECTIONS

1. Heat oven to 250°F. Cut open pumpkin and scoop out seeds and pulp.

2. Transfer seeds to large bowl of water. Spoon out loose seeds that float and separate pulp from remaining seeds. Discard pulp. You should have about 2 cups seeds.

3. Transfer seeds to colander and rinse. Drain, then pat dry with dishtowels.

4. Spread cleaned seeds on baking sheet and bake until dry, about 1 hour.

5. Increase oven temp to 350°F. Toss seeds with olive oil, season with salt and roast, tossing occasionally, until golden brown and crisp, 20 minutes.

PER SERVING: About 210 calories, 19 g fat (3 g saturated), 10 g protein, 60 mg sodium, 3.5 g carbohydrates, 2 g fiber

TRY THIS

Add the additional ingredients along with the olive oil and salt in step 5, and roast as directed in the recipe.

Cacio e Pepe: ½ cup finely grated Romano cheese, 2 teaspoons pepper

Sweet Heat: ¼ cup brown sugar, ⅛ teaspoon cayenne

Apple Snacks with Almond Butter and Pomegranate

ACTIVE TIME: 5 MINUTES ✄ **TOTAL TIME: 5 MINUTES** ✄ **MAKES 1 SERVING**

INGREDIENTS

½ apple, sliced into 2 rounds

3 tablespoons almond butter

1 tablespoon pomegranate seeds

½ teaspoon chia seeds

DIRECTIONS

1. Spread apple slices with almond butter and sprinkle with pomegranate and chia seeds.

PER SERVING: About 360 calories, 27 g fat (2 g saturated), 11 g protein, 5 mg sodium, 24 g carbohydrates, 8 g fiber

Green Matcha Popcorn

ACTIVE TIME: 5 MINUTES ✄ **TOTAL TIME: 5 MINUTES** ✄ **MAKES 6 SERVINGS**

INGREDIENTS

1 tablespoon confectioners' sugar

2 teaspoons matcha tea powder

5 cups air-popped popcorn

DIRECTIONS

1. Whisk together sugar and matcha powder. In large bowl, toss with popcorn.

PER SERVING: About 30 calories, 0.5 g fat (0.05 g saturated), 1 g protein, 1 mg sodium, 6.5 g carbohydrates, 0.3 g fiber

TRY THIS Popcorn is a fantastic blank canvas for seasoning. Try furikake (Japanese seasoning blend), nutritional yeast, powdered sugar and cinnamon, or taco seasoning.

For a quick and substantial snack, spread ¼ cup Classic Hummus on 1 pita. Top with 2 thin slices red onion, separated; 2 tablespoons crumbled feta cheese; and a pinch of pepper. Drizzle with 1 teaspoon extra virgin olive oil. Toast until crisp around the edges, and top with basil leaves.

Classic Hummus

ACTIVE TIME: 15 MINUTES ✕ **TOTAL TIME: 1 HOUR 20 MINUTES, PLUS OVERNIGHT SOAK** ✕ **MAKES 14 SERVINGS (3½ CUPS)**

INGREDIENTS

- 1 cup dried chickpeas
- 1 teaspoon baking soda
- 4 cloves garlic, peeled
- 6 tablespoons fresh lemon juice
- ¾ teaspoon salt
- ¾ teaspoon ground cumin
- ¾ cup tahini
- ¼ cup water

DIRECTIONS

1. In 4-quart saucepan, add dried chickpeas, baking soda and enough cold water to cover by 2 inches. Let stand at room temp overnight, then drain (do not rinse) and return to pot along with enough cold water to cover by 2 inches. Bring to a boil. Reduce heat to medium and simmer 1 hour, or until chickpeas are soft and skins have loosened.

2. In food processor or blender, pulse garlic, lemon juice, salt and ground cumin until chopped. Add tahini and water, then pulse until smooth. Drain the cooked chickpeas and add to tahini mixture, then process until smooth, stopping and stirring occasionally. Store in airtight container in fridge for up to 2 weeks.

PER SERVING: About 135 calories, 8 g fat (1 g saturated), 5 g protein, 110 mg sodium, 12.5 g carbohydrates, 2.5 g fiber

TRY THIS

Cardamom-Ginger: Stir 1 tablespoon grated peeled fresh ginger and ½ teaspoon ground cardamom into Classic Hummus recipe.

Roasted Pepper and Mint: Finely chop ¾ cup each packed fresh mint and roasted red peppers with 2 tablespoons capers and stir into Classic Hummus recipe.

Sweet and Spicy Nuts

ACTIVE TIME: 15 MINUTES ✕ **TOTAL TIME: 40 MINUTES** ✕ **MAKES 32 SERVINGS (8 CUPS)**

INGREDIENTS

- 1 cup sugar
- 2 teaspoons salt
- 1 teaspoon ground cumin
- 1 teaspoon ground cinnamon
- 1 teaspoon pepper
- ½ teaspoon cayenne
- 1 large egg white
- 6 cups unsalted nuts (such as pecans, almonds, walnuts and cashews)

DIRECTIONS

1. Heat oven to 325°F. Grease two 10½- by 15½-inch jelly-roll pans.

2. In small bowl, combine sugar, salt, cumin, cinnamon, pepper and cayenne; stir until blended. In large bowl, with wire whisk, beat egg white until foamy. Add nuts to egg white and stir to coat evenly. Add sugar mixture and toss until nuts are thoroughly coated.

3. Divide nut mixture between prepared jelly-roll pans, spreading evenly. Bake, stirring twice during baking, until golden brown and dry, 25 to 27 minutes. With slotted spoon, transfer nuts to waxed paper and spread in single layer. Cool. Store in airtight container at room temp for up to 1 month.

PER SERVING: About 175 calories, 13 g fat (2 g saturated), 5 g protein, 125 mg sodium, 12 g carbohydrates, 2 g fiber

Grab-and-Go Cranberry Granola Bars

ACTIVE TIME: 15 MINUTES ✕ **TOTAL TIME: 45 MINUTES** ✕ **MAKES 16 SERVINGS**

INGREDIENTS

- 2 cups old-fashioned oats
- ½ cup honey
- ½ cup vegetable oil
- 2 tablespoons water
- 2 large egg whites
- 2 tablespoons packed light-brown sugar
- 1 teaspoon ground cinnamon
- ½ teaspoon salt
- ¾ cup wheat germ, toasted
- ¾ cup chopped walnuts
- ¾ cup dried cranberries

DIRECTIONS

1. Heat oven to 325°F. Spray a 9- by 13-inch metal baking pan with nonstick cooking spray. Line pan with foil, leaving a 2-inch overhang, and spray foil. Set aside.

2. Spread oats on a plate and microwave on High, in 1-minute intervals, for 4 to 5 minutes or until fragrant and golden, stirring occasionally. Let cool.

3. In large bowl, whisk honey, oil, water, egg whites, sugar, cinnamon and salt until well blended. Fold in oats, wheat germ, walnuts and dried cranberries. Transfer to prepared pan. Using wet hands, press into even layer.

4. Bake 28 to 30 minutes or until golden. Cool in pan on wire rack. Using foil, transfer to cutting board and cut into 16 bars.

PER SERVING: About 220 calories, 12 g fat (1 g saturated), 4 g protein, 70 mg sodium, 27 g carbohydrates, 3 g fiber

MAKE AHEAD Store the bars up to four days in an airtight container at room temp, or up to one month in the freezer.

Choco-Cherry Granola Bars

ACTIVE TIME: 15 MINUTES ✖ TOTAL TIME: 1 HOUR 15 MINUTES ✖ MAKES 14 SERVINGS

INGREDIENTS

- 2 cups old-fashioned oats
- ½ cup quinoa
- ½ cup chia seeds
- ½ cup sliced almonds
- ½ cup dried cherries
- ½ cup chopped dark chocolate
- ¾ cup creamy almond butter
- ⅓ cup honey
- 2 tablespoons coconut oil
- ½ teaspoon salt
- ½ cup pureed prunes (from about 1 cup whole prunes)

DIRECTIONS

1. Line large baking sheet with parchment paper.

2. In large bowl, combine oats, quinoa, chia seeds, almonds, cherries and chocolate.

3. In small saucepan on low, heat almond butter, honey, coconut oil and salt until melted and smooth, stirring occasionally. Stir in prune puree.

4. Pour almond butter mixture over oat mixture and stir to combine.

5. With hands, form into bars using about ⅓ cup mixture for each; place on prepared sheet and refrigerate until set, about 1 hour. Store in refrigerator in airtight container for up to 3 weeks.

PER SERVING: About 300 calories, 17 g fat (4 g saturated), 7 g protein, 105 mg sodium, 35 g carbohydrates, 6 g fiber

TRY THIS

Swap cumin, chile powder or
garlic powder for paprika.

Paprika Parmesan Granola Bars

ACTIVE TIME: 10 MINUTES ✸ **TOTAL TIME: 40 MINUTES** ✸ **MAKES 8 SERVINGS**

INGREDIENTS

- 1 cup rolled oats, toasted
- ½ cup crisp rice cereal
- ½ cup grated Parmesan
- ½ cup freeze-dried vegetable bits
- ⅓ cup smoked almonds, chopped
- 3 tablespoons chia seeds
- ½ teaspoon smoked paprika
- ½ teaspoon salt
- ½ teaspoon pepper
- 2 large egg whites, beaten
- ½ cup unsweetened nut butter

DIRECTIONS

1. Heat oven to 350°F. Line an 8-by-8-inch metal pan with foil, then grease the foil. Combine oats, rice cereal, Parmesan, freeze-dried vegetables, almonds, chia seeds, paprika, salt and pepper. Stir in egg whites and unsweetened nut butter. Press firmly into pan.

2. Bake for 30 minutes. Cool completely on a wire rack. Remove from pan and cut into 8 bars. Store in airtight container at room temp up to 1 week.

PER SERVING: About 235 calories, 2 g fat (1 g saturated), 10 g protein, 305 mg sodium, 18 g carbohydrates, 5 g fiber

MEAL PLANS

WEEK 1

	Sunday	Monday	Tuesday
Breakfast	Sheet-Pan Pancake with Blueberry Syrup, page 51	Mini Sesame Zucchini Loaves	Super-Simple Summer Smoothies, page 52 (double the recipe and freeze the leftovers for smoothie pops for Saturday)
Lunch	Chickpea and Kale Soup, page 84	Chickpea and Kale Soup	Five-Spice Beef Stew
Snack	Zucchini Tots, page 195	¼ cup mixed nuts and an apple	Chickpea "Nuts"
Dinner	Five-Spice Beef Stew, page 91	Mustard-Crusted Mini Meatloaves, page 135, and roasted potatoes and carrots (see Vegetable Roasting Guide on page 27)	Butternut Squash and White Bean Soup, page 71 (peel and chop 2 butternut squash—use ¼ for the soup and reserve the rest for Friday dinner)
Prep	• Make Mini Sesame Zucchini Loaves (page 49) and refrigerate	• Prepare Chickpea "Nuts," page 196	

The meal plans that follow will give you four weeks' worth of ideas. Use them as a guideline, adjusting as necessary for the size of your family (you might need to double a recipe) or your meal prep style (you can do much or all of the prep work on one weekend day, for example). The blue shading in the meal plans indicates leftovers or meals that use pre-prepped ingredients.

Wednesday	Thursday	Friday	Saturday
Sheet-Pan Pancake with Blueberry Syrup	Mini Sesame Zucchini Loaves	Milk and Honey Overnight Chia	Tuscan Sausage and Kale Frittata, page 61
Butternut Squash and White Bean Soup	Grain bowl with leftover Roasted Squash Couscous Salad (See **Easy as 1, 2, 3: Grain Bowls**, page 180)	Chicken and Red Plum Salad, page 105, with leftover Moroccan Roast Chicken	Butternut Mole Enchiladas
¼ cup mixed nuts and an apple	Zucchini Tots	Chickpea "Nuts"	Smoothie pops
Mustard-Crusted Mini Meatloaves with Roasted Squash Couscous Salad, page 97 (make enough couscous salad to have some for Thursday's lunch)	Moroccan Roast Chicken, page 141, with green salad (make enough chicken to have some for Friday lunch) • Prepare Milk and Honey Overnight Chia, page 56	Butternut Mole Enchiladas, page 179, with a side of rice	Grain or noodle bowl using leftovers (See **Easy as 1, 2, 3: Grain Bowls**, page 180)

WEEK 2

	Sunday	Monday	Tuesday
Breakfast	Best-Ever Granola, page 55, with yogurt	Spring Herb Frittata	Best-Ever Granola with yogurt
Lunch	Peanutty Edamame and Noodle Bowl, page 173	Pulled pork sandwiches with leftover carnitas	Spiced Fresh Tomato Soup with Sweet and Herby Pitas
Snack	Apple Snacks with Almond Butter and Pomegranate, page 201	Paprika Parmesan Granola Bars	Apple Snacks with Almond Butter and Pomegranate
Dinner	Carnitas Tacos, page 125	Grilled Chicken Kebabs, page 163 and roasted vegetable of choice (see Vegetable Roasting Guide on page 27)	Steak with Kale and White Bean Mash, page 133 (cook an extra 3 steaks for tomorrow's lunch and Thursday dinner)
Prep	• Make a big pot of white beans (see No-Fail Dry Beans, page 30) to use for Tuesday dinner and Thursday lunch • Make Paprika Parmesan Granola Bars, page 209, and store in an airtight container • Prep Spring Herb Frittata, page 65, for easy baking on Monday morning	• Prepare Spiced Fresh Tomato Soup with Sweet and Herby Pitas, page 69 (make enough soup to have some for Tuesday lunch and Wednesday dinner) • Prepare White Bean Mash, page 133, for Tuesday dinner	• Roast cauliflower for tomorrow's salad (see roasting instructions on page 95)

Wednesday	Thursday	Friday	Saturday
Spring Herb Frittata	Overnight Steel-Cut Oats	Super-Simple Summer Smoothie, page 52	Breakfast Burritos, page 59 (use any leftovers from Sweet Potato Tacos)
Kale and Roasted Cauliflower Salad, page 95, topped with leftover steak	White Bean and Tuna Salad, page 99, with prepared dressing and white beans	Sweet Potato, Avocado and Black Bean Tacos, page 122, with prepared sweet potatoes (use white beans if you have leftovers)	Loaded Sweet Potatoes, page 187 (use white beans if you have leftovers)
Paprika Parmesan Granola Bars	Apple Snacks with Almond Butter and Pomegranate	Paprika Parmesan Granola Bars	Best-Ever Granola with yogurt
Spiced Fresh Tomato Soup with grilled cheese sandwiches	Asian Steak Noodle Bowl, page 137, with prepared steak	Hearty Bean and Beef Chili, page 89	Soup using leftovers (See **Easy as 1, 2, 3: Freestyle Soups**, page 76)
• Prepare Overnight Steel-Cut Oats, page 57 • Prepare the dressing for White Bean and Tuna Salad, page 99 (double the recipe to use for Thursday and Saturday lunch)	• Roast sweet potatoes for Friday lunch (see roasting instructions on page 122)		

	Sunday	Monday	Tuesday
Breakfast	Tuscan Sausage and Kale Frittata, page 61	Make-Ahead Egg and Cheese Sandwiches	Pumpkin-Cherry Breakfast Cookies
Lunch	Spring Minestrone, page 73	Tuscan Sausage and Kale Frittata	Spring Minestrone
Snack	¼ cup mixed nuts and an apple	Classic Hummus with crudités for dipping	Grab-and-Go Cranberry Granola Bars
Dinner	Pork Tenderloin with Quinoa Pilaf, page 113 (make extra quinoa and store for dinner Monday night and lunch Wednesday)	Crispy Tofu Bowl, page 175, with leftover quinoa	Sheet-Pan Chickpea Chicken, page 165 (cook extra chicken for Wednesday lunch and Thursday dinner)
Prep	• Cook, assemble, and freeze Make-Ahead Egg and Cheese Sandwiches, page 60 • Cook big batch of chickpeas (see No-Fail Dry Beans, page 30) • Make Classic Hummus, page 203	• Make Pumpkin-Cherry Breakfast Cookies, page 53 • Make Grab-and-Go Cranberry Granola Bars, page 205	• Assemble Mexican Beef Meatballs with Chipotle Sauce, page 134, and arrange (uncooked) on a foil-lined baking sheet. Cover and refrigerate.

Wednesday	Thursday	Friday	Saturday
Make-Ahead Egg and Cheese Sandwiches	Pumpkin-Cherry Breakfast Cookies	Choco-Cherry Granola Bars	Mint Pesto Baked Eggs
Chicken Quinoa Bowls, page 151, with leftover chicken and quinoa	Meatball pitas with Mexican Beef Meatballs with Chipotle Sauce	Creamy Lemon Pasta with Chicken and Peas	White Bean Cassoulet with Pork and Lentils
Classic Hummus with crudités for dipping	Grab-and-Go Cranberry Granola Bars	Classic Hummus with crudités for dipping	¼ cup mixed nuts and an apple
Mexican Beef Meatballs with Chipotle Sauce with brown rice (see Grain Cooking Guide on page 33)	Creamy Lemon Pasta with Chicken and Peas, page 153	White Bean Cassoulet with Pork and Lentils, page 87 (double recipe and freeze second portion for another week)	Tacos using leftovers (See **Easy as 1, 2, 3: Tacos**, page 126)
	• Make Choco-Cherry Granola Bars, page 207	• Prep Mint Pesto Baked Eggs, page 56	

WEEK 4

	Sunday	Monday	Tuesday
Breakfast	Mushroom Ragu and Polenta Egg Bake, page 63 (make extra ragu)	Spiced Plum and Quinoa Muffins	Breakfast Burritos
Lunch	Wild Mushroom Risotto, page 183, with green salad	Pasta with leftover Mushroom Ragu	Quick 'n' Easy Empanadas
Snack	Green Matcha Popcorn, page 201	Sweet and Spicy Nuts	Green Matcha Popcorn
Dinner	Cuban-Style Pulled Pork with Olives, page 114	Quick 'n' Easy Empanadas, page 115, with sautéed onions and peppers	Sausage and Broccoli Quinoa Bowl
Prep	• Bake Spiced Plum and Quinoa Muffins, page 47 • Chop peppers for Monday and Wednesday dinner • Make Sweet and Spicy Nuts, page 204	• Assemble and freeze Breakfast Burritos, page 59 • Roast sausage and broccoli and cook quinoa for Sausage and Broccoli Quinoa Bowl, page 117	

Wednesday	Thursday	Friday	Saturday
Spiced Plum and Quinoa Muffins	Breakfast Burritos	Spiced Plum and Quinoa Muffins	Overnight Steel-Cut Oats
Sausage and Broccoli Quinoa Bowl	Curried Chicken Salad Wraps, with prepared chicken salad	Grain bowl topped with leftover chicken salad	Crispy Caprese Cakes, page 84, made with leftover Mushroom Risotto from Monday, and served with green salad
Sweet and Spicy Nuts	Easy Yogurt Dip with crudités	Fruit of choice	Easy Yogurt Dip with crudités
Fennel Roasted Chicken and Peppers, page 139	20-Minute Cauliflower Soup, page 85, with avocado toasts	Beef and Pineapple Kebabs with Cashew Rice, page 131	Fried rice with leftover rice plus any leftovers from the week's meals
• Make chicken salad for Curried Chicken Salad Wraps, page 166, with leftover chicken • Make Easy Yogurt Dip, page 193		• Assemble Overnight Steel-Cut Oats, page 57	

	Sunday	Monday	Tuesday	Wednesday	Thursday	Friday	Saturday
Breakfast							
Lunch							
Snack							
Dinner							
Prep							

INDEX

HEARST HOME

Cover and book design by Girl Friday Productions

Library of Congress Cataloging-in-Publication Data Available on Request

10 9 8 7 6 5 4 3 2 1

Published by Hearst Home, an imprint of Hearst Books
Hearst Magazine Media, Inc.
300 West 57th Street
New York, NY 10019

For information about custom editions, special sales, premium and corporate purchases, please go to hearst.com/magazines/hearst-books

Printed in China
ISBN 978-1-950785-22-3

PHOTO CREDITS

Cover: Mike Garten

Interior: All photos by Mike Garten except where noted.

Yossy Arefi: 26; Danielle Occhiogrosso Daly: 44, 58, 66, 68, 70, 72, 74, 82, 86, 94, 98, 102, 104, 106, 112, 116, 126, 130, 132, 136, 150, 152, 156, 162, 164, 172, 174, 188; Kate Whitaker: 140

Getty Images: 1, natthanim; 19, Armando Rafael; 25, Maximilian Stock Ltd.; 41, Annabelle Breakey; 77, Cavan Images

Icons (NP: Noun Project / SS: Shutterstock): Pot (Throughout), Realstockvector/SS; Diet (Throughout), Sudowoodo/SS; Fried Egg (45), Michael Loupos/NP; Bowl (67), ArtWorkLeaf/NP; Plate (111), Khurasan/NP; Apple (191), Vectorstall/NP